# STAR WARS

## THE FORCE AWAKENS

### THE VISUAL DICTIONARY

Heat-sensitive
cranial palp

Venom-laced teeth of
great strength

Dexterous
forelimb

WORRT

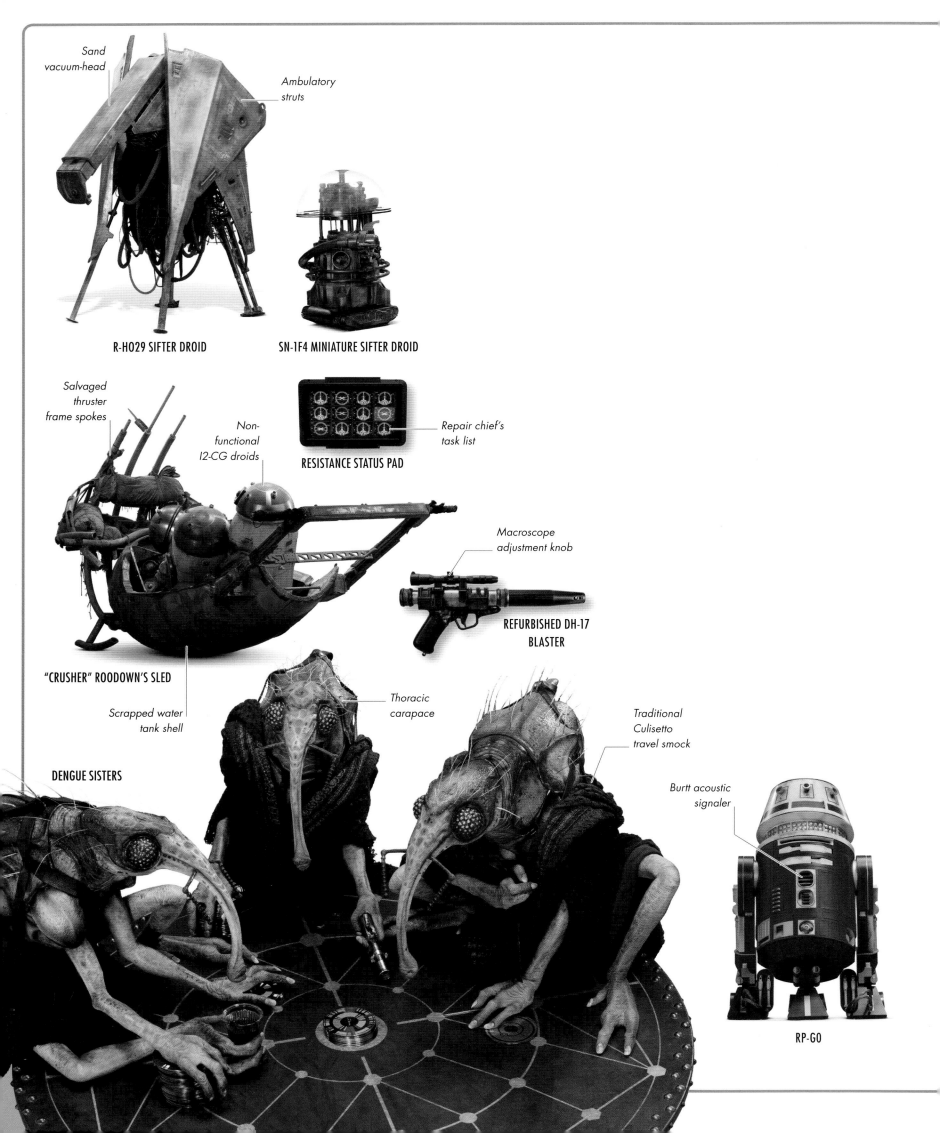

Sand vacuum-head

Ambulatory struts

RP-GO

**R-HO29 SIFTER DROID**

**SN-1F4 MINIATURE SIFTER DROID**

Salvaged thruster frame spokes

Non-functional I2-CG droids

Repair chief's task list

**RESISTANCE STATUS PAD**

Macroscope adjustment knob

**REFURBISHED DH-17 BLASTER**

**"CRUSHER" ROODOWN'S SLED**

Scrapped water tank shell

Thoracic carapace

Traditional Culisetto travel smock

Burtt acoustic signaler

**DENGUE SISTERS**

RP-GO

# STAR WARS

## THE FORCE AWAKENS

### THE VISUAL DICTIONARY

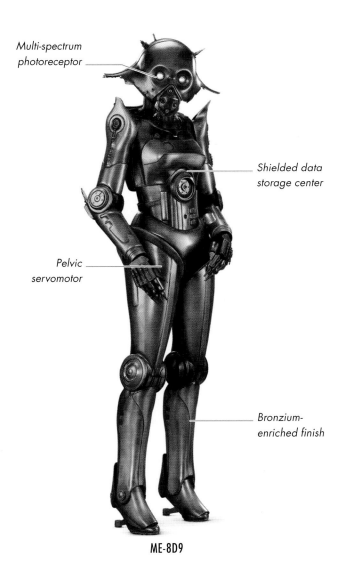

Multi-spectrum
photoreceptor

Shielded data
storage center

Pelvic
servomotor

Bronzium-
enriched finish

ME-8D9

**REY'S WATER
BOTTLE**

**TRAINING REMOTE**

Shock ray
emitter

**WRITTEN BY PABLO HIDALGO**
SPECIAL FABRICATIONS BY JOHN GOODSON

# CONTENTS

| | |
|---|---|
| Introduction | 6 |
| Peace Interrupted | 8 |
| BB-8 | 10 |
| Poe Dameron | 12 |
| Lor San Tekka | 14 |
| Stormtroopers | 16 |
| Flametroopers | 18 |
| FN-2187 | 20 |
| Finn | 22 |
| Kylo Ren | 24 |
| Kylo Ren: Dark Warrior | 26 |
| Captain Phasma | 28 |
| Rey | 30 |
| Rey: Survivor's Spirit | 32 |
| Starship Graveyard | 34 |
| Niima Outpost | 36 |
| Unkar Plutt | 38 |
| General Hux | 40 |
| Finalizer Crew | 42 |
| TIE Fighter Pilots | 44 |
| Han Solo | 46 |
| Chewbacca | 48 |
| Rathtars | 50 |
| Guavian Death Gang | 52 |
| Kanjiklub | 54 |
| General Organa | 56 |
| Resistance Commanders | 58 |
| Resistance Pilots | 60 |
| Resistance Ground Crew | 62 |
| C-3PO | 64 |
| R2-D2 | 65 |
| The Senate | 66 |
| Starkiller Base | 68 |
| Snowtroopers | 70 |
| Maz Kanata | 72 |
| Maz's Castle | 74 |
| Castle Guests | 76 |
| Index | 78 |
| Acknowledgments | 80 |

# INTRODUCTION

***STAR WARS: THE FORCE AWAKENS*** launches audiences
into a new era of storytelling. A New Republic holds sway over
a civilized galaxy. In the depths of uncharted space, the next
evolution of the Empire—the First Order—stands ready to unleash
destruction on an unsuspecting target. The Resistance, outnumbered
and underequipped, is all that stands in its way. Absent from the
galactic stage are the Jedi Knights—Luke Skywalker is missing
when the galaxy seems to need him the most. It falls to a new
generation of heroes to rise and rekindle the power of the Force.

The gap of 30 years since the events of *Return of the Jedi* invites
endless speculation as to what has happened since that triumph
of the Rebel Alliance over the evil Galactic Empire. How has the
galaxy reshaped itself? Who are the players in this latest struggle
for power? What has become of the legends of the past and
who are the new heroes of tomorrow? This Visual Dictionary starts
to answer some of those questions.

# PEACE INTERRUPTED

**AFTER YEARS OF REBELLION,** the death of Emperor Palpatine gave the oppressed peoples of the galaxy undeniable evidence that the Empire could be defeated. A longing for freedom and peace drove a great tide of revolution from sector to sector, to the point where a truce—unthinkable at the height of the Galactic Civil War—was signed between the New Republic and the weakened Empire. As one of its first acts, the restored Senate promptly passed the Military Disarmament Act. Many were convinced that the age of galaxy-wide conflict was over.

## THE NEW REPUBLIC

Following its great victory against the Empire at the Battle of Endor, the Alliance to Restore the Republic rebranded itself as the New Republic, and shortly afterward a peace treaty—the Galactic Concordance—was signed with the remnants of the Empire. Believing that the Empire was no longer a threat, the New Republic turned its attention to reshaping galactic politics.

## THE FIRST ORDER

The Galactic Concordance defanged the Empire's ability to wage war, with strict disarmament treaties and punishing reparations. The Old Empire withered away, becoming a remnant of political hardliners locked in a cold war with the New Republic, before eventually breaking away to reform in the Unknown Regions as the mysterious First Order.

## THE RESISTANCE

The Resistance is a small private force created by Princess Leia Organa to keep watch on the movements of the First Order. Though she petitions the New Republic government for support, she finds the politics of the Senate too slow and too mired in self-interest to be of any help. The New Republic tolerates the Resistance, though it is wary of risking war with the First Order.

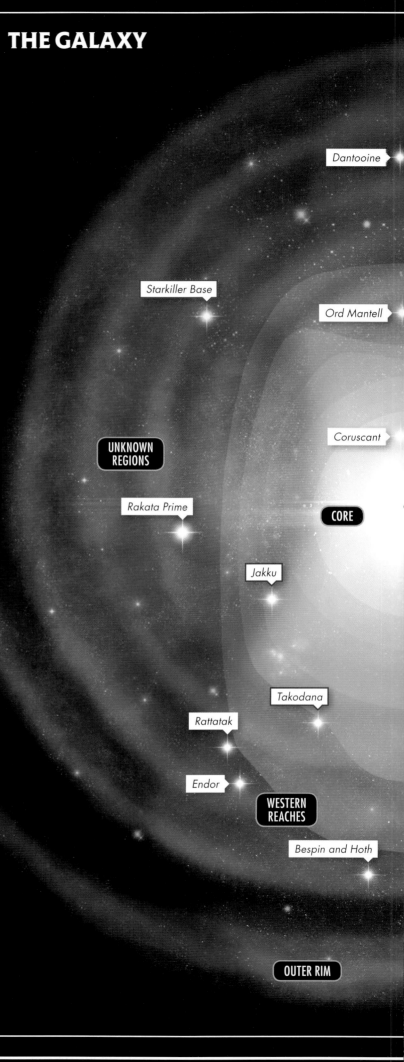

**THE GALAXY**

Dantooine

Starkiller Base

Ord Mantell

UNKNOWN REGIONS

Coruscant

Rakata Prime

CORE

Jakku

Takodana

Rattatak

Endor

WESTERN REACHES

Bespin and Hoth

OUTER RIM

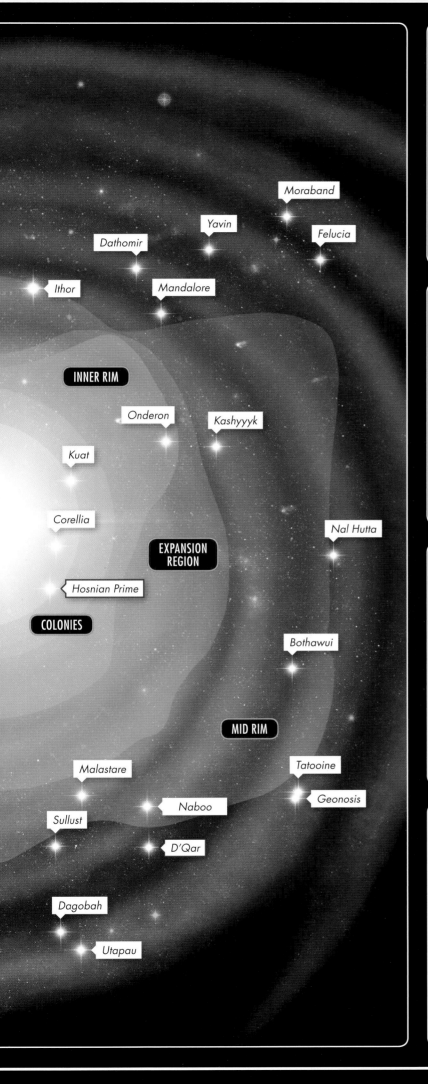

Moraband

Yavin

Felucia

Dathomir

Ithor

Mandalore

**INNER RIM**

Onderon

Kashyyyk

Kuat

Corellia

Nal Hutta

**EXPANSION
REGION**

Hosnian Prime

**COLONIES**

Bothawui

**MID RIM**

Malastare

Tatooine

Geonosis

Naboo

Sullust

D'Qar

Dagobah

Utapau

## HOSNIAN PRIME

To demonstrate that the New Republic was not doomed to repeat the errors of the past, one of Chancellor Mon Mothma's first edicts was the restoration of the Galactic Senate, to create a forum where the Republic would define its very nature. It was decided that all worlds would have an equal say in the shaping of government. This change resulted in the capital of galactic politics moving from Coruscant, its home for millennia. Member worlds would now host the Senate on a rotating basis. At this time, it is the cosmopolitan world of Hosnian Prime where the Senate convenes.

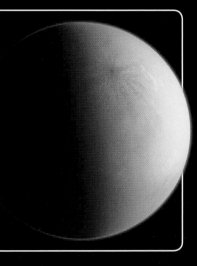

## JAKKU

Jakku is a striking example of a world shaped by the aftermath of the Galactic Civil War. The barely settled desert world in the Western Reaches became a rallying point for retreating Imperial forces, and they fought a last-stand battle above the planet, which once held a secret Imperial research base. A huge fleet of New Republic warships engaged Imperial vessels in the upper atmosphere, and the crippled Imperial ships used their tractor beams to drag Republic vessels into the sands below. The end result was a vast graveyard of warships, waiting to be plundered.

## TAKODANA

Galactic Republic, Imperial, New Republic—who is in charge of the galaxy matters little to the most cynical of space pirates, who look to make a living on the edges of the law and civilized space. Takodana has been a haven for shady spacers for centuries, as the den of famed pirate Maz Kanata. In her castle keep she hosts a crossroads for travelers looking to journey deeper into civilization or farther into the frontier. War has not come to Takodana, as it has remained neutral throughout its long history, and spies on all sides frequent Maz's castle, hoping to find strategic information.

## D'QAR

A world of lush vegetation and no native intelligent life, D'Qar fit the profile for a prospective rebel base when it was first scouted decades earlier by members of Corona Squadron. Pilots Thane Kyrell and Kendy Idele initially surveyed the world for signs of an Imperial presence prior to the Battle of Endor. A small Alliance outpost was later established, but the war ended before the need for a full-scale base ever surfaced. The scouting report remained secure in Alliance records for when the Resistance required a hidden base of operations.

# BB-8

**AN INTENSELY LOYAL** astromech droid, BB-8 is usually never far from pilot Poe Dameron's heels. Like the older, larger astromechs that assist the ranks of the Resistance starfighter forces, BB-8 is equipped to control the flight and power distribution systems of a starfighter when the droid is locked into its astromech socket. The pairing of a selenium power drive and a dedicated, goal-focused personality keeps this orbiculate automaton tirelessly rolling, even into certain danger.

Though BB-8's self-preservation protocols result in the droid being skittish and easily frightened, its experiences have created a strong loyalty subprogram that cannot be overwritten.

Magnetic caster

Commutator

Ollisteep-4D nanopin data port

Service access thread

Stainless inoxium

Lightweight cranial frame

Towerslee-15 accelerometer

High frequency receiver antenna (damaged)

Condensed helical transmitter antenna

## TRUSTY COMPANION

BB-8 is the first to spot the approaching First Order invasion of Kelvin Ravine on Jakku, and attempts to warn Poe. As it becomes clear that Poe is unable to complete his mission for General Leia Organa, the pilot asks BB-8 to continue alone. The little droid bravely evades the attacking stormtroopers and rolls into the foreboding desert night.

## ALWAYS MOVING

An internal orbiculate motivator rolls BB-8's body, while its head is kept perched atop the sphere with magnetic casters. Wireless telemetry between the head and body removes the need to keep the head tethered to a single contact point. When BB-8 needs extra stability or must traverse areas it can't roll through, it fires compressed liquid cable launchers that then reel the droid into hard-to-reach spots.

Primary photoreceptor

Articulated holoprojector array

BB-8's dense shell and sealed access points prevent dust contamination that would have seized the servomotors of older models.

Power recharge port

Motivator
cooling vents

Surface sensors

## DATA FILE

› BB-8 converses in 27th generation droidspeak code, a compressed variant of the most common astromech language.

› BB-8's tracking mode, which connects it to the Resistance network, was neglectfully disabled prior to its latest mission.

## FRIENDS IN FLIGHT

Poe Dameron grew up hearing tales of heroic pilots and their trusty astromechs, and as such has always fostered a deep respect for his droid companions. Dameron keeps BB-8's systems up to date and the droid's mechanical components well maintained. BB-8 returns the favor by making sure the settings on any ship assigned to Poe are configured to his preferences.

BB-8's six swappable circular tool-bay disks can be replaced and upgraded with minimal reprogramming. This example is equipped with a magnetic-tipped bolt-spinner.

# POE DAMERON

**POE DAMERON GREW UP** hearing the legends of the starfighter jockeys of old, having been raised by veterans of the Rebel Alliance. At 32 years old, Poe is now the most daring and skilled of the Resistance pilots. His appetite for risk is indulged by even the most serious minded Resistance commanders, as he gets spectacular results when pitted against First Order starfighter patrols. Though brash, Poe has great charisma and limitless respect for the idealistic founders of the Resistance, particularly his idol, General Leia Organa.

## REBEL ROOTS

Poe Dameron was born toward the explosive finale of the war between the Rebel Alliance and the Galactic Empire. His mother, Shara, was an Alliance fighter pilot while his father, Kes, also served in the rebel military. Poe was raised on Yavin 4, in a newly established colony not far from the Massassi ruins from which the Rebel Alliance launched the fateful mission that destroyed the first Death Star.

## MISSION TO JAKKU

Massively outnumbered by the First Order, the Resistance scrapes together what resources it can to prepare for the oncoming war. General Organa sends Poe to the poorly settled fringes of the galaxy's Western Reaches, where he seeks out Lor San Tekka. This old ally of Leia and her brother holds information that can save the Resistance.

As Poe gets ready to depart Tuanul village in Kelvin Ravine on Jakku, he witnesses the approach of First Order invaders and impulsively rushes into action.

Flight jacket with non-regulation tailoring

Stock with gas reservoir

Macroscope adjustment controls

Sealed blaster lasing chamber

Removable galven-circuitry barrel tip

Security access plate

Electroshock discharge generator

Trigger guard

### POE'S BLASTER RIFLE

A BlasTech EL-16HFE (Heavy Field Edition) blaster rifle is cradled within a charging slot inside Poe's X-wing cockpit. A model used throughout the Resistance, it is outdated New Republic surplus.

Resistance commander ground uniform

### FIRST ORDER BINDERS

Weatherproofed adventurer boots

Reckless Poe has been in many tight spots throughout his adventures, but even he is helpless before the overwhelming power commanded by Kylo Ren, enforcer of the First Order.

## DATA FILE

> In addition to his skills as a pilot, Poe is a capable infantryman, equipped with gear such as Neuro-Saav TE4.4 field quadnoculars.

> Poe has been flying starships since he was six years old.

# RESISTANCE ACE

Poe served as a squadron leader in the New Republic Defense Fleet, but was frustrated by the central government's failure to take the First Order threat seriously. Upon being recruited into the Resistance, Poe found an organization that better resembled the Rebel Alliance of old. He quickly rose through the ranks of the Resistance's understaffed Starfighter Corps, earning the grade of commander. If the Resistance had recruitment posters, Poe's fellow pilots joke that he would triple their numbers with his dashing bravado alone.

Long-range laser cannon
BB-8
Armored cockpit module
Nose cone housing sensor array
Fusial thrust engine
Scissor-split S-foil

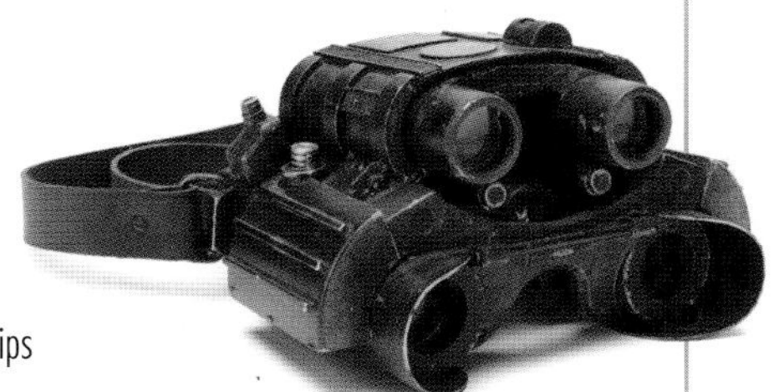

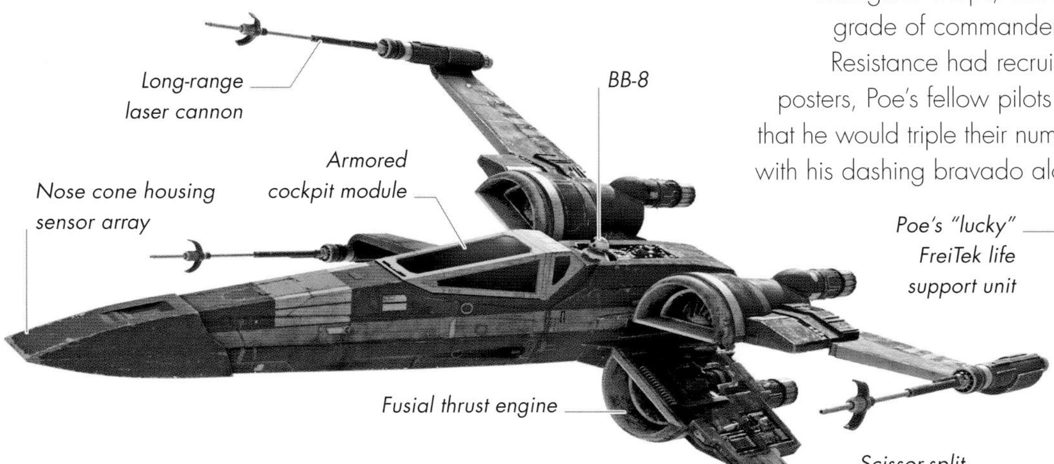

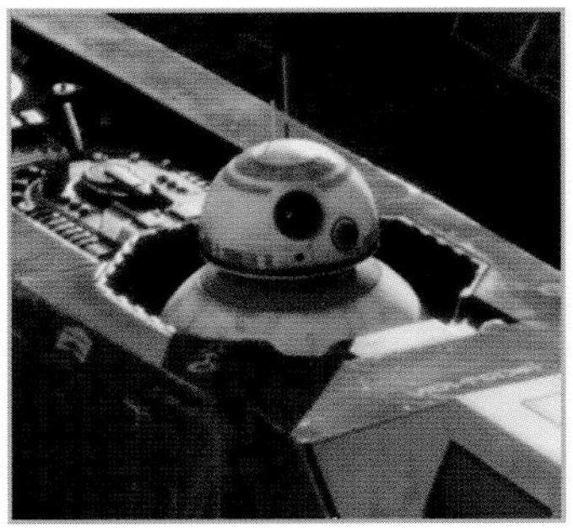

**CUSTOMIZED X-WING**
Poe's *Black One* is a customized Incom-FreiTek T-70 X-wing fighter coated with sensor-scattering ferrosphere paint. Though often overlooked by sensors, the colors certainly stand out to the organic eye. BB-8 considers *Black One* the best and smoothest ride of Poe's ships.

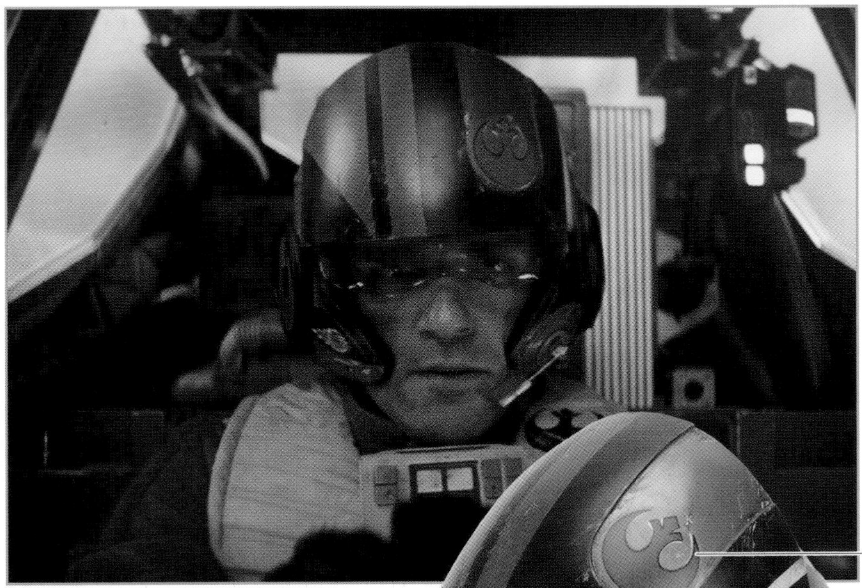

Though many starfighter pilots detest atmospheric missions, Poe delights in soaring through skies and skimming the surfaces of planets. The tug of the wind creates an intense and turbulent feedback that feeds Poe's appetite for thrills.

Old Rebel Alliance symbol has been adopted by the Resistance
Anti-corrosion lacquer finish

**POE'S HELMET**

Tousled hair from wearing helmet
Inflatable flight vest
Poe's "lucky" FreiTek life support unit
Glie-44 blaster pistol

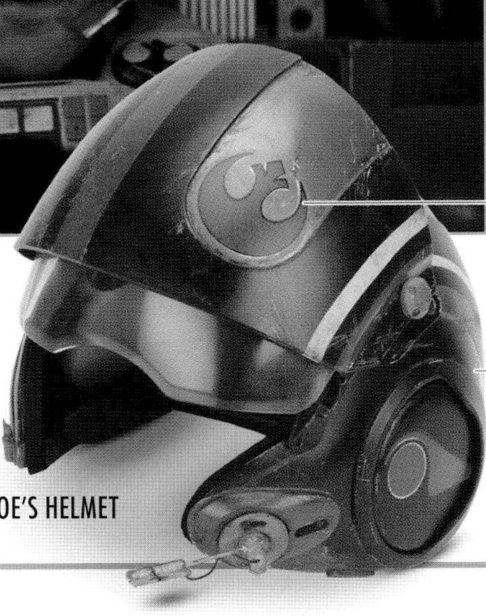

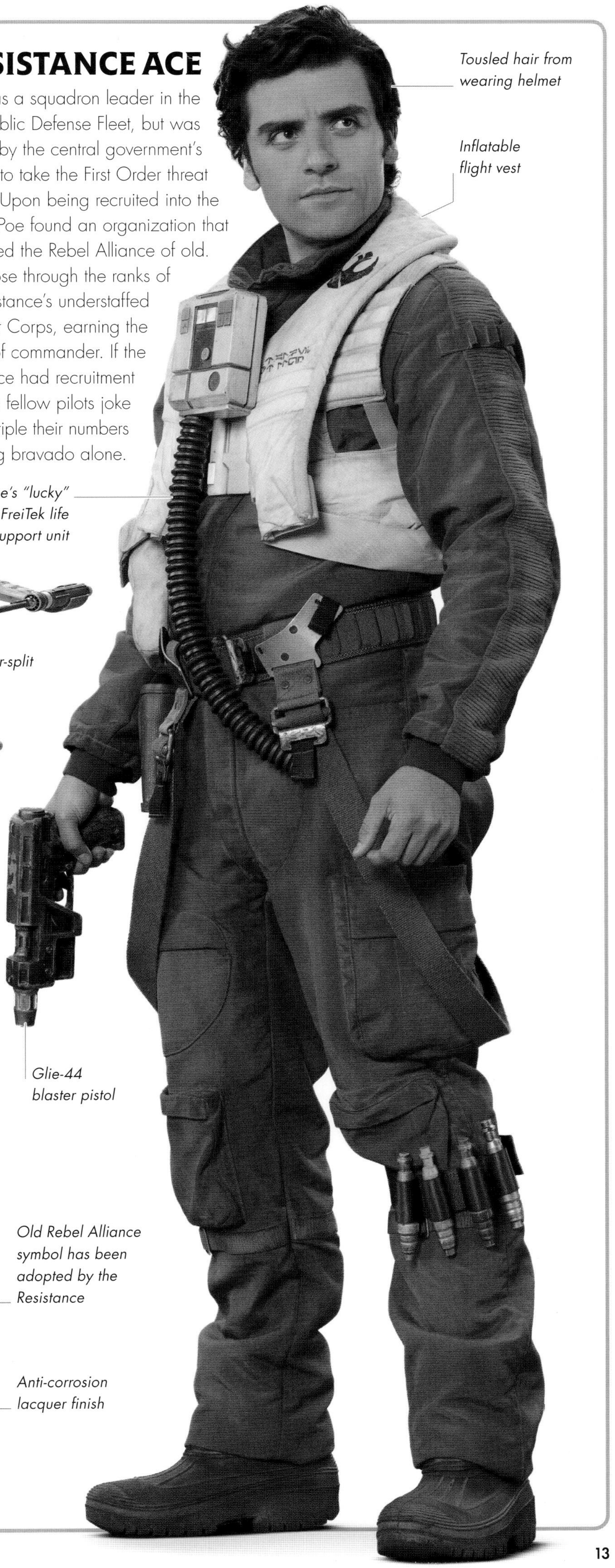

# LOR SAN TEKKA

AS THE EMPIRE TOPPLED, retreating Imperial officials destroyed records that would have been vital to the New Republic's attempts at galactic reconstruction. New Republic bureaucrats turned instead to firsthand accounts from well-traveled locals to fill in the gaps. A seasoned traveler and explorer of the more remote fringes of the galaxy, Lor San Tekka has proven his worth to the New Republic and the Resistance many times over. Ready to retire after decades of exploration and adventure, the spiritual San Tekka has settled with a colony of villagers in the remote Kelvin Ravine on the frontier world of Jakku.

*Home-spun fantabu-wool coat*

*Chain of Wisdom*

Knowing that Lor San Tekka is a font of obscure information, Poe Dameron seeks him out on Jakku, hoping that his esoteric knowledge will be of benefit to the Resistance.

*Tuanulberry-dyed linen tunic*

## DATA FILE

> Lor travels lightly and shows wisdom in the few artifacts he continues to carry from place to place.

> Lor is old enough to have witnessed the Jedi Knights prior to the Clone Wars. He never believed the lies that painted them as traitors.

*Gundark-hide survival belt*

In his travels, Lor San Tekka uncovered much of the history of the Jedi Knights that the Galactic Empire had tried so hard to erase. Others now seek him for his knowledge of Jedi secrets.

**CHERISHED ARTIFACT**
Hidden in a plain leather sack is Lor's most valued possession—an antiquated data storage unit.

## KEEPER OF FAITH

Though San Tekka is not Force-sensitive, he has witnessed its power firsthand. During the dark times of Emperor Palpatine's rule, San Tekka was a follower of the Church of the Force. This underground faith was made up of loosely affiliated worshippers of the Jedi ideals, who steadfastly believed that one day their light would return to the galaxy.

# VILLAGER ESSENTIALS

The villagers of Tuanul follow an ascetic lifestyle, rejecting the comforts and luxuries of the galaxy. Even in matters of defense, the villagers prefer to create their own weapons rather than line the coffers of weapons manufacturers. Though not pacifists, the villagers reject the trappings of warfare, especially the profit-driven conflicts that have polluted much of the galaxy.

**MACES**

**PICKAX**

**BLOGGIN-OIL LAMP**

**SHOVEL**

**AX**

*Salvaged industrial power shunt*

**ILCO MUNICA'S BLASTER RIFLE/CLUB**

**DASHA PROMENTI'S BLASTER PISTOL**

*Carved dune zaywar tusk handle*

Seeking Lor San Tekka, the First Order sends more than sixty stormtroopers to pacify Tuanul village, which the villagers fight tenaciously to defend.

Built around a large vaporator cistern, the wattle and daub huts of Tuanul village are an oasis of life in the otherwise empty Kelvin Ravine.

*Pump-action recharger*

*Weighted stock doubles as war club*

**ILCO MUNICA**

*Abednedo species*

*Unadorned hair*

*Fantabu-fur fringed vest*

*Pilgrim's robe*

*Sash of the Balanced*

*Insulated boots*

*Simple dyed linen dress*

**DASHA PROMENTI**

# TUANUL VILLAGERS

In the time of the Empire, with the Sith secretly in command of the galaxy, any displays of organized worship or belief in the supernatural were against Imperial law. Underground religions spread across the galaxy, to finally emerge from the shadows with the defeat of Emperor Palpatine. Tuanul village on Jakku houses a collective of worshippers who praise the virtues of the Force without being graced by the ability to wield it.

# STORMTROOPERS

**THE FOOT SOLDIERS** of the First Order draw upon the heritage of the armored infantry units that blazed across the battlefields of the Clone Wars, in the final years of the Old Republic. The stark white armor that was once an honorable symbol of defense was transformed under the Empire into the faceless icon of an evil regime. Treaty stipulations forbade the building and mobilization of stormtrooper forces after the Galactic Civil War, but little does the New Republic realize that the First Order is escalating its military preparations for a bold strike. Stormtroopers once again are leading the charge.

Though the conflict between the First Order and its enemies has not yet escalated into full-scale war, there have been isolated skirmishes as the First Order tests the New Republic's resolve.

## TRAINING REGIME

During the time of the Galactic Empire, inconsistent academy standards led to stormtroopers of varying skill and ability. Out of necessity, the First Order enforces a far more regimented approach to training to ensure excellence across its reduced stormtrooper ranks. First Order stormtrooper training emphasizes improvisation and counter-insurgency operations, as well as guerrilla tactics. No longer tasked with ensuring loyalty to a dominant galactic government, these soldiers instead need to know how to claw their way back into power. This mindset has created a more well-rounded combat education than the training of the past.

*Composite betaplast helmet with integral polarized lenses*

*Filtration system with external tank hook-up*

*Web gear holds extra ammunition*

*Sonn-Blas FWMB-10 repeating blaster—also known as a megablaster*

### DATA FILE

> To keep their weight down, most stormtrooper helmets lack advanced imaging gear, requiring stormtroopers to use separate quadnoculars in the field.

> Stormtroopers are denied any form of identification beyond their serial numbers.

**Barrel cooling shroud**

# CLOSE COMBAT

Worlds within First Order territory are ruled with cruel authority, and stormtroopers are the first line of punishment for anyone who needs to be reminded of this. To suppress unruly civilians, stormtroopers are trained in riot control tactics and assigned specialized non-lethal equipment to batter their opponents into submission.

**Lightweight composite betaplast ballistic riot shield**

**Collapsible conductor contact vanes**

**Z6 RIOT CONTROL BATON**

**Adhesion grip magnatomically pairs with trooper gloves**

**Spotlight**

**Cockpit**

## TROOP TRANSPORTER

The Atmospheric Assault Lander (AAL) ferries up to 20 stormtroopers (2 squads) from an orbital carrier to a combat site quickly and precisely, avoiding anti-ship fire long enough to deploy its forces.

**Landing gear**

**Disembarkation ramp**

**Lethal force used if riot situations escalate**

# ADVANCED ARSENAL

To avoid the treaty restrictions that prevented major galactic corporations from selling arms to the First Order, BlasTech Industries and Merr-Sonn Munitions cynically spun off a subsidiary called Sonn-Blas Corporation, which operates within First Order space. This company manufacturers the majority of First Order weaponry, building on classic templates that date back to the Clone Wars. Modern stormtrooper weaponry boasts precision manufacture, rugged designs, and efficient energy cells for greater battlefield accuracy, ammunition yields, and operational lifespan.

**Heat dispersing barrel head**

**Integrated sight and mounting bracket**

**SONN-BLAS SE-44C BLASTER PISTOL**

**Vibrating pulser warns of low ammunition**

**Adjustable J19 electroscope**

**SONN-BLAS F-11D BLASTER RIFLE**

**Power cell**

**Improved joint design allows greater flexibility than Imperial-era armor**

**Removable stock assembly**

**Magnatomic adhesion grip with integrated power feed indicator**

**Collapsible steadying grip**

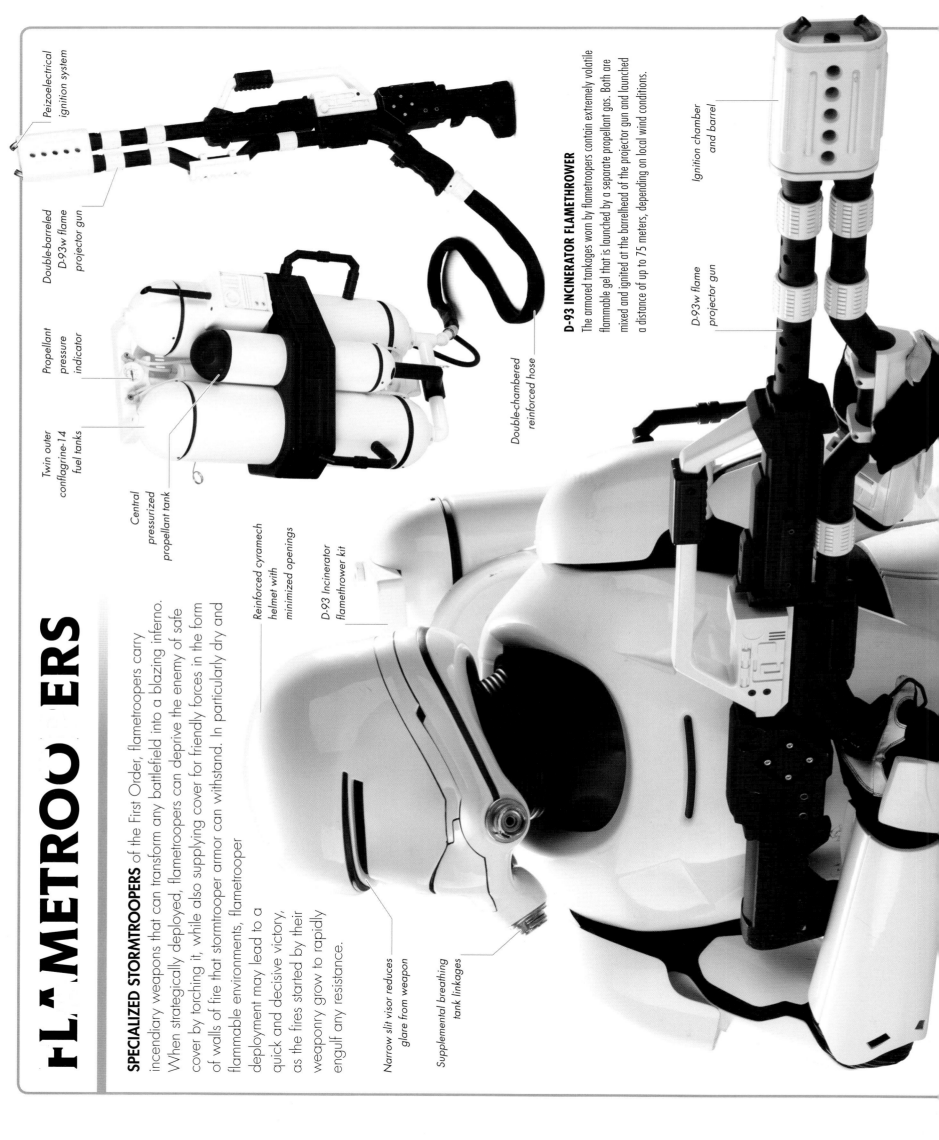

# FLAMETROOPERS

**SPECIALIZED STORMTROOPERS** of the First Order, flametroopers carry incendiary weapons that can transform any battlefield into a blazing inferno. When strategically deployed, flametroopers can deprive the enemy of safe cover by torching it, while also supplying cover for friendly forces in the form of walls of fire that stormtrooper armor can withstand. In particularly dry and flammable environments, flametrooper deployment may lead to a quick and decisive victory, as the fires started by their weaponry grow to rapidly engulf any resistance.

Peizoelectrical ignition system

Double-barreled D-93w flame projector gun

Propellant pressure indicator

Twin outer conflagrine-14 fuel tanks

Central pressurized propellant tank

Double-chambered reinforced hose

Reinforced cyramech helmet with minimized openings

D-93 Incinerator flamethrower kit

Narrow slit visor reduces glare from weapon

Supplemental breathing tank linkages

## D-93 INCINERATOR FLAMETHROWER

The armored tankages worn by flametroopers contain extremely volatile flammable gel that is launched by a separate propellant gas. Both are mixed and ignited at the barrelhead of the projector gun and launched a distance of up to 75 meters, depending on local wind conditions.

Ignition chamber and barrel

D-93w flame projector gun

Standard ten-soldier stormtrooper squads contain a slot for a single weapons specialist. Depending on mission profiles, that specialist may be a megablaster heavy assault trooper, a riot control trooper, or a flametrooper. The soldiers sent to raid Jakku consist of representatives of all of these types.

## DATA FILE

> Incendiary weapons are a millennia-old infantry mainstay, modernized by the Mandalorian supercommandos and the Republic clone troopers of the Clone Wars.

> Common Resistance nicknames for flametroopers include "roasters," "hotheads," and "burnouts."

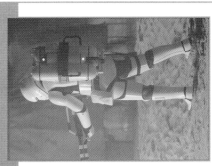

*Heat deflecting armored gaiters*

*Articulated greaves allow for greater foot movement*

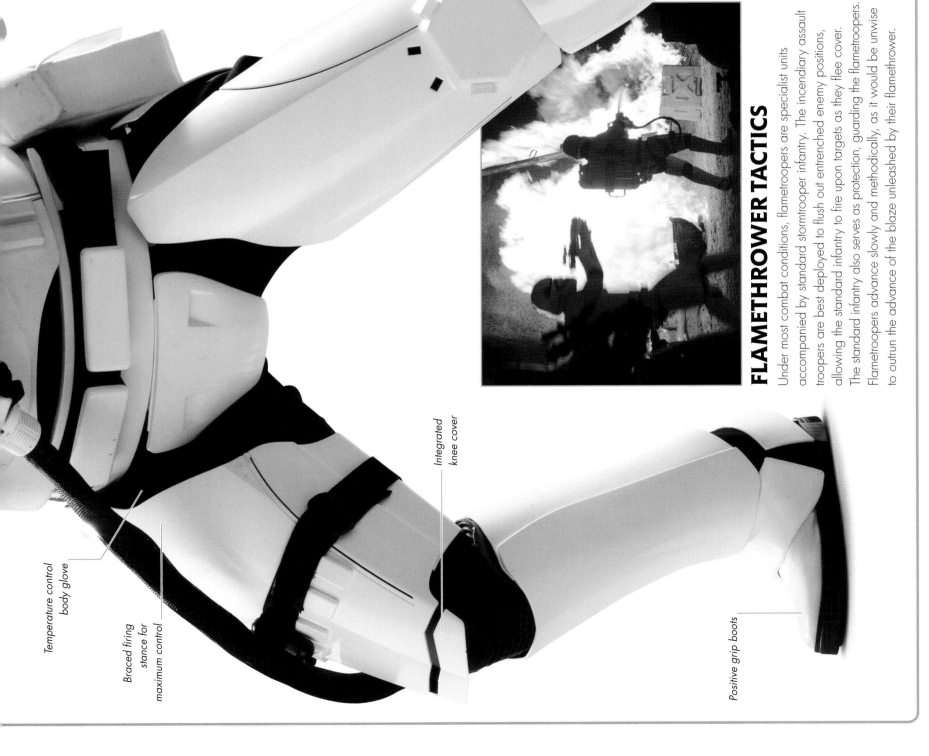

*Temperature control body glove*

*Braced firing stance for maximum control*

*Integrated knee cover*

*Positive grip boots*

# FLAMETHROWER TACTICS

Under most combat conditions, flametroopers are specialist units accompanied by standard stormtrooper infantry. The incendiary assault troopers are best deployed to flush out entrenched enemy positions, allowing the standard infantry to fire upon targets as they flee cover. The standard infantry also serves as protection, guarding the flametroopers. Flametroopers advance slowly and methodically, as it would be unwise to outrun the advance of the blaze unleashed by their flamethrower.

# FN-2187

**A PRODUCT OF THE** First Order's methodical, systemized military training programs, FN-2187 proves to be a highly skilled stormtrooper—at least, during simulations. Though FN-2187's agility, endurance, coordination, and accuracy score high marks, he lacks the combat zeal or submission to authority evident in his squadmates. FN-2187 keeps his misgivings well hidden. Before his first combat assignment, his record is free of any signs of dissent. His spotless profile does not survive a brutal night assault on a sacred village on Jakku.

*Glossy betaplast finish requires constant cleaning*

*Hand print with FN-2003's blood*

*23 standard years spent training (from birth)*

*Pauldron armor plate*

### STORMTROOPER HELMET

The standard infantry helmet of the First Order protects FN-2187's head, equips him with communications and targeting systems, and conceals any shred of individuality.

*Rerebrace armor plate*

FN-2187 quickly learns the terrible reality of war during the Jakku raid, when he witnesses the sudden and violent death of his squadmate FN-2003.

*F-11D blaster rifle*

*FN-2187's vivid combat simulations do not prepare him for such horrible scenes as the cold-blooded massacre of innocent civilians.*

*Features data recording and target-lock for artillery, airborne, or orbital strikes*

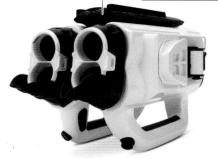

### STORMTROOPER QUADNOCULARS

Quadnoculars are oversized image enhancers used by First Order stormtroopers. The quartet of precision lenses offer enhanced multispectral imaging.

## RELUCTANT WARRIOR

While FN-2187 performs at the top of his combat classes, the ever-present First Order propaganda never really takes hold in his heart. FN-2187's motives to excel are personal, not political—he is more concerned with protecting his squadmates than bringing order to the galaxy. He has a friendly, charming personality that conceals just how unprepared he is for life outside the First Order.

Used to relying on his fellow troopers, FN-2187 finds himself instinctively pairing with and trusting strangers rather easily.

# GREAT ESCAPE

After the terrible events on Jakku, FN-2187 resolves to escape from First Order service. He releases the imprisoned Resistance pilot, Poe Dameron, and the pair recklessly steals a Special Forces TIE fighter. Despite Poe's best efforts, First Order weapon batteries shoot the craft down, but FN-2187 is able to eject from the doomed vessel and parachute to relative safety.

## DATA FILE

> FN-2187's unit is under the direct command of Captain Phasma, who monitors his performance closely.

> As part of his training rotation, FN-2187 also logged many hours on sanitation detail, dirty work that nonetheless needed doing.

*Seat restraints*

*Weapon selection toggle controls*

*Emergency rations beneath seat (FN-2187 is unaware of this)*

**TIE FIGHTER EJECTOR SEAT**

*Explosive launcher mechanism*

Fast-talking FN-2187 enlists the aid of beleaguered Poe Dameron in his hastily conceived escape plan. Used to improvisation, Poe agrees, knowing he has few options available.

FN-2187 awakens in the Sinking Fields of the Goazon Badlands on Jakku. He is amazed to be alive, but dismayed when he finds no sign of Poe.

## CRASH SITE

As sturdy as the Special Forces TIE fighter may be, it was never meant to survive such a hard landing. The vessel is a crumpled, smoldering wreck, soon swallowed by the shifting sands of the Sinking Fields.

*FN-2187 will discard his armor to avoid detection*

*Shattered port solar array*

# FINN

**AFTER THE RAID** on Jakku, questions arise regarding FN-2187's competence on the battlefield. He is scheduled to undergo "renewal therapy" to ensure his unquestioning loyalty to the First Order, but before that happens, FN-2187 has a profound change of heart, and becomes a fugitive. He adopts the name "Finn" instead of his numerical designation, the only identity he has ever known. It would seem that Finn's good nature—a gentleness, humor, and unerring moral compass—could not be wiped from his mind as it is from others who undergo stormtrooper training.

Tortured by thirst on Jakku, Finn drinks from a trough shared by a stinking happabore. No simulation could prepare him for the hardships of desert survival.

*Resistance fighter jacket, "borrowed" from Poe Dameron*

The First Order's determination to capture BB-8 as well as recover a deserter turns life upside down for Rey, who is swept up in Finn's escape.

Covering his frantic flight from Jakku, Finn puts his training to good use behind the controls of the *Millennium Falcon*'s vintage Corellian AG-2G quad laser cannons.

## DESERTER

Once the rush of escape fades and Finn has a moment to collect his thoughts, he begins to realize the enormity of his actions. Having made an enemy of Kylo Ren means Finn must keep running. Knowing very little of the galaxy's workings beyond the borders of the First Order, Finn at first considers joining a pirate crew. But such thoughts instantly vaporize when the First Order strikes again, and reveals the unrivaled power of its ultimate weapon— a weapon that Finn served in the shadow of.

Removable collimating barrel tip

Gas cartridge

**FINN'S BLASTER**

Improvised thermal detonator

**PYRO DENTON EXPLOSIVE**

Having shed his First Order equipment, Finn picks up an older Resistance blaster rifle offered to him by Han Solo. The BlasTech EL-16 is similar enough to the stormtrooper F-11D for Finn to use well.

Fierce devotion to newfound friends

Irising aperture to adjust bolt spread

Self-sealing combat mesh fabric

Carry strap

## DATA FILE

> Despite Finn's sheltered upbringing, he has heard of Han Solo (as an Alliance general) and Luke Skywalker (as a Jedi Knight).

> Finn nearly joins the crew of pirate Captain Ithano while on Takodana.

Finn strives to make himself useful while on the Resistance base. His lifetime of First Order training means he is a natural at sorting ordnance.

Stormtrooper temperature-control body glove

## RESISTANCE FIGHTER

Finn has little knowledge of galactic politics. His sheltered upbringing within the First Order would have resulted in a skewed view of history, had he bothered paying attention to the propaganda. Though Finn may not fully appreciate the aims and struggles of the Resistance, he does value friendship. Seeing that the cause of the Resistance is one that matters deeply to Poe Dameron, Han Solo, and Rey, Finn signs up, even though his past may cause some in the Resistance to distrust him.

Weatherproof underboots

Finn's firsthand knowledge of the First Order proves extremely valuable to the efforts of Rey and Han Solo.

# KYLO REN

**STRIDING ONTO RAVAGED BATTLEFIELDS** with bold purpose, his singed robes whirling about his lean frame, is the mysterious Kylo Ren. His body radiates with suppressed anger, a fiery temper kept in check and honed to a deadly point. Though Ren often arrives after his stormtroopers have secured victory, he has no fear of battle. His ability to use the Force grants him many impressive combat skills, but Kylo Ren is no Jedi, nor is he a Sith. He is the archetype of a new generation of dark side users that have emerged to fill the void left by the Sith's demise.

## DATA FILE

> Kylo Ren is an adopted name; his birth name is never spoken, by decree of the First Order's Supreme Leader.

> The Supreme Leader believes Ren to be the ideal embodiment of the Force, a focal point of both light and dark side ability.

## INTERROGATION

Resistance Commander Poe Dameron, captured while trying to uncover a trove of Jedi information, undergoes questioning.

To ensure the First Order remains unchallenged, Kylo Ren has been tasked with hunting down any remnants of the Jedi. The dark warrior employs torture on his helpless captives, using a disturbing array of pain-inflicting devices. Beyond such tools, Kylo is skilled at using the Force to probe the minds of the unwilling, tearing loose deeply held secrets.

*Articulated restraint plastron*

*Vital sign monitoring sensors*

*Arm restraints*

### INTERROGATION CHAIR
Similar to devices developed by the Inquisitorius of the Galactic Empire, Kylo Ren's interrogation chair is a collection of pain-causing implements distributed along a prisoner-confining frame.

*Electroshock conduit*

**INTERROGATION TOOLS**

Within his private quarters aboard the *Finalizer*, Kylo Ren communes with the charred remnants of Darth Vader, vowing to finish the work the Dark Lord started a generation earlier.

*Silver inlay radiates from the eyes as a symbol of power*

*Hinged mechanism seals tightly when shut*

*Empty socket where transparisteel holoplate rested*

## KYLO REN'S HELMET

Patterned after the battle gear of the Knights of Ren, Kylo Ren's helmet conceals his identity and adds to his imposing demeanor. Servomotors drive articulated arms that separate the face mask from the helmet, letting Kylo remove the black form to stare down his opponents with uncontained malice.

*Integrated vocabulator projects Ren's voice*

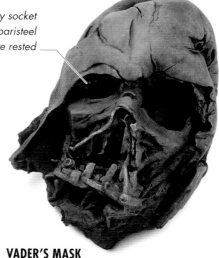

### VADER'S MASK
Scavenged from a funeral pyre on Endor, Darth Vader's charred and melted helmet is a silent symbol of both the dark side's power and its weakness.

Cowl is a remnant from
Ren's early training

Cape singed from
multiple battles

Turbolaser
battery

Tractor beam
projectors

Central
flight deck

### THE *FINALIZER*

Constructed in a secret shipyard
within the Unknown Regions, the
*Finalizer* is a clear violation of New
Republic disarmament treaties.

## COMMAND SHIPS

Kylo Ren commands from the bridge of the *Finalizer*, a *Resurgent*-
class Star Destroyer bristling with firepower. At nearly 3,000
meters long, it is almost twice the size of the Old Empire's Star
Destroyers. For travel to planetary surfaces, Kylo uses an *Upsilon*-
class shuttle, with towering wings that cut an imposing profile.
The crews of both ships know to be wary of Ren's volatile temper.

### REN'S SHUTTLE

The shuttle's enormous stabilizer wings
serve as deflector shield projection and
sensor surfaces, providing the ship with
impressive data collection capabilities
and resistance to incoming fire.

Wings are articulated
to slant outward in
flight configuration

Unstable
serrated
plasma blade

Twin heavy
laser cannon

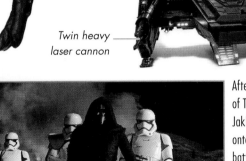

After the subjugation
of Tuanul village on
Jakku, Kylo Ren emerges
onto the smoldering
battlefield to personally
interrogate any
high-value prisoners.

## FIRST ORDER WARRIOR

Kylo Ren exists outside the formal command structure
of the First Order, and has a direct link to the
shadowy Supreme Leader who is ultimately in charge of these
forces of darkness. It is with palpable tension that the upper
command of the First Order contends with Kylo, as his
agenda always trumps military objectives. In this way, Kylo's
placement within the hierarchy resembles that of Darth Vader
in the old Galactic Empire. This is entirely by design.

# KYLO REN: DARK WARRIOR

**HAVING STUDIED JEDI SKILLS** as well as arcane dark side lore, Kylo Ren is the embodiment of conflict, drawing upon contradictory teachings and deriving power from discord. Ren has taken pains to bury his past, though he uses the unpleasant emotions that stir within him when reflecting upon his youth to fuel his anger and dark powers. Through his veins courses the bloodline of the most powerful Jedi and Sith, and Ren sees it as his birthright to rule the weaker beings in the galaxy. As his power rises, it eclipses his past life leaving the young man further isolated. Kylo Ren aspires to build immunity to the light side—to succeed where Darth Vader and his sentimentality once failed.

Unstable plasma blade matrix

Battered combat helmet

Crudely assembled hilt that mirrors ancient design

Kylo Ren is the most gifted apprentice of Supreme Leader Snoke, a mysterious figure steeped in dark side knowledge who commands the First Order from a distance.

## LIGHTSABER COMBAT

The lightsaber skills of Kylo Ren are, ironically, responsible for that elegant weapon and its combat forms remaining unknown to the galaxy at large. Kylo Ren betrayed the other Jedi students studying with Master Luke Skywalker, and is responsible for their destruction. He has well earned the nickname "Jedi Killer," whispered in the First Order ranks, as it was his deadly lightsaber skill that prevented the return of the Jedi Order.

Padded armor

Quillon plasma blade

Kylo uses taunts and psychological attacks

Accusing finger reinforces unquestioned authority

Cracked kyber crystal

Vent iris opens just after primary blade ignition

Crossguard vent shroud

Harmonic energizer conductive plate

Crystal cradle

Power cell focusing shunt

Hand gestures help visualize Force techniques

Power cell brace

Power field conductors

## KYLO'S LIGHTSABER

Kylo Ren's unusual lightsaber is an ancient design, dating back thousands of years to the Great Scourge of Malachor. The crossguard blades, or quillons, are tributaries of the primary central blade, all spawning from a cracked kyber crystal that is the cause of their ragged, unstable appearance. An array of focusing crystal activators split the plasma stream into perpendicular blade energy channels, creating the quillons. The emitter shrouds on the crossguard protect the bearer's hand from the smaller blades.

Central diatium power core

Exposed power rod terminals

Reserve power cell

## THE DARK SIDE

The dark side flows through Kylo Ren, making him an almost unstoppable force on the field of battle. His reflexes and telekinetic defenses are immense—he is able to stop an incoming blaster bolt in midair and hold it in place for several seconds before releasing it. He is also a master of telepathic intrusion, using the ability to coerce or torment his prisoners into revealing secret information.

Inert power insulator

Cooling vanes

The crossguard blades emerge soon after the main blade snaps into existence, helping to balance the power of Kylo Ren's lightsaber.

# CAPTAIN PHASMA

Brushed chromium crown with comlink transmission planes

Traditional cape of First Order command

Polarizing lenses with integral MFTAS (Multi-Frequency Targeting Acquisition System)

Vocodor speaker ports

## CHARGED WITH COMMANDING

**CHARGED WITH COMMANDING** the stormtrooper forces of the First Order, Phasma's true rank is higher than the simplistic label "captain" would suggest. Although her position could easily afford her a well-appointed war room far from the battlefield, Phasma insists on seeing combat operations firsthand, and shuns any comfortable trappings of elevated rank. She wears distinctive chromed armor that broadcasts her authority, but also makes clear that she is a woman of action who fights alongside those under her command.

Phasma disagrees with General Hux over what it takes to make a soldier. The methodical Hux has developed automated training regimes that simulate battle situations. Phasma believes such programs don't test the true heart of a soldier: courage and tenacity.

## STORMTROOPER COMMANDER

Despite the intensely patriotic First Order records of the Empire's military effectiveness, Phasma privately concedes the shortcomings of its original stormtroopers. She believes it was the interference of politics—and shortsighted, ambitious Imperial officials—that led to soldiers of uneven skill and effectiveness. Phasma looks to guard against such meddling. She sees it as her duty to ensure that only the best soldiers wear the armor of the First Order, and that their numbers aren't wasted on trivial assignments.

Modified precision-crafted crush gauntlets

Mid-torso mounted ammunition holders

Phasma's armor is coated in salvaged chromium from a Naboo yacht once owned by Emperor Palpatine. Its polished finish helps reflect harmful radiation, but it serves primarily as a symbol of past power.

## PHASMA IN COMBAT

Phasma has led from the front as the First Order expands into the wilderness of the Unknown Regions. Obsessed with physical perfection, she spends every waking hour honing her combat abilities. She is a qualified expert on all First Order small arms, and has also trained in vehicular and starfighter combat. She pays little heed to outdated notions of inequality between genders, an idea common on undeveloped worlds. To her thinking, a female stormtrooper is nothing new at all. The anonymity provided by their armor concealed the fact that both men and women served the Galactic Empire as stormtroopers.

*Armorweave cape with First Order colors*

*Segmented sabatons*

*Chromium finish*

**PHASMA'S BLASTER RIFLE**

*Pistol grip*

*Macroscope sight gives eight-power magnification and low-light capability*

*Recurved trigger guard for two-handed grip*

*Extensible stabling grip for long range sniping*

A perfectionist, Phasma routinely patrols the areas under her command as a means of keeping her senses keen and her soldiers in line. Even in such an expansive operation as Starkiller Base, Phasma makes most of these inspection rounds on foot, walking dozens of kilometers in a typical day.

# REY

**LIFE ON JAKKU** is tough—it is a daily struggle for survival on the harsh planet. Nineteen-year-old Rey has carved out her existence on this bleak frontier world. Each day she has marked her victory over the searing sunlight, scorching sands, and cutthroat scavengers with a scratch along the wall of her makeshift home. Thousands of scratches are a testament to her tenacity and survivor's instinct. Despite a life that should have built a barrier against any sympathy or weakness, Rey still possesses a generous heart and a willingness to help those in need.

*Skin has adapted to extreme UV radiation*

*Tight bindings keep out the sun and sand*

### REY'S HOUSE

Rey lives in a toppled AT-AT walker, not far from the junkfields that surround Niima Outpost. A hatch in the walker's exposed belly leads to the sloping interior that Rey calls home. Here, she refurbishes scrap prior to trading it, and sleeps in a simple hammock.

*X-wing pilot helmet once belonging to Captain Dosmit Ræh of the Tierfon Yellow Aces*

Rey crafted this Alliance pilot doll when she was 10 years old, from debris she found in the junkfields.

*Orange fabric salvaged from a New Republic cargo container*

**DOLL**

**SALVAGED REBEL FLIGHT HELMET**

*Satchel holds tools and small salvage*

## LIVING ALONE

Rey is a gifted mechanic, seemingly having an innate sense of how machinery fits together and functions. Having grown up in the shadows of last-generation war technology, she is comfortable around vehicles and weapons. She has also become a skilled pilot, despite showing no desire ever to leave her desolate world. Her only escapes from the brutal conditions of Jakku are vivid flights of imagination, where she envisions lush, green worlds and fantasizes about a family she has never known.

Rey has maintained the weatherproofing on her toppled AT-AT in excellent condition, keeping the desert heat out during Jakku's scorching day, and the warmth in on chilly nights. Traps keep other scavengers out of her home.

# SCAVENGER

Rey's daily routine on Jakku consists of treks into the junkfields, where she explores inside the massive wrecks, scavenging valuable pieces of technology. She brings her haul to Niima Outpost, where she trades it for food. Climbing through decaying Star Destroyers or Star Cruisers requires Rey to be in peak physical shape, and she must also be ready to defend herself against cutthroat thieves who roam the wastes.

Rey's vehicle favors speed over cargo capacity, meaning she must often make return trips to carry salvage into town. Rey has seen that smaller hauls are easier to defend; a greedy scavenger quickly draws rivals.

Goggles are stormtrooper helmet lenses

Salvaged quarterstaff

Primary heat exchanger

Netting filled with salvage

Windscreen

Vertical stabilizer

Afterburner assembly

Survival equipment stored inside

## REY'S SPEEDER

Rey's junker speeder is a cobbled-together transport that she built for travel across the Jakku wilderness. The craft sits between the classifications of speeder bike and swoop, not quite fitting in either category. A modified tractor web keeps Rey in place as the speeder rockets up to immense speeds, and well-positioned heat sinks keep the engine thrusters from burning her.

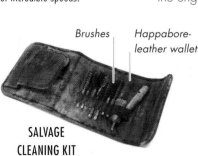

The forward intake grill directs air into a dual turbojet assembly, producing turbocharged thrust for incredible speeds.

Mesh-windowed salvage sack

Brushes

Happabore-leather wallet

Water bottle

**SALVAGE CLEANING KIT**

**SURVIVAL SATCHEL**

Govath-wool traveler's boots

Tools

Compressed air tank

**SALVAGE TRAY**

# REY:
## SURVIVOR'S SPIRIT

**REY'S RECOGNITION** of the importance of the Resistance's survival in the face of the rising First Order threat gives her the strength to leave Jakku. She joins Finn on his inherited mission to deliver BB-8 to a Resistance stronghold. Though she still harbors ideas of returning to Jakku, Rey is catapulted into an adventure that makes it clear her fate lies along a path far from that dead-end desert world. Her skills as a warrior, pilot, and mechanic are fully tested, and Rey comes to discover she has remarkable abilities she never suspected.

Rey has learned self-defense as a matter of necessity. With her battered but durable staff, she has perfected thrusting, swinging, and striking techniques to keep away unruly thugs.

## A TOUGH LIFE

Rey's skills as a scavenger have earned the respect of many junk traders, particularly Unkar Plutt, who orders his thugs not to steal her wares as she is much more valuable as a continued source of salvage. When Rey oversteps this fragile respect by reneging on a trade with Plutt, the temperamental junk boss orders that she be taught a violent lesson. This is far from the only betrayal she has suffered. The harsh conditions on Jakku have taught Rey that good fortune often invites trouble, and bullies only fear strength.

*Firm back arm grip to power a sudden swing*

*Heat exchanger plate*

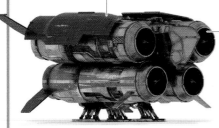

*Quadrijet fusial thrust intake*

*Salvaged quarterstaff*

### QUADJUMPER
Berthed in Bay 3 at Niima Outpost, this Quadjumper belongs to a group of independent junk haulers and arms dealers. First Order TIE fighters blast it to cinders when Rey and Finn briefly consider using the ship as an escape craft.

*Bloggin-leather and wool strap*

*Blade fashioned from droid arm attachment*

### REY'S KNIFE

*Lower defensive position*

*Agile footwork practiced on shifting sands*

Having made an enemy of the First Order by her alliance with Finn, Rey is forced to flee Jakku. She and Finn hurriedly board a dilapidated Corellian freighter, and Rey proves her remarkable piloting abilities.

# AN AWAKENING

Since the disappearance of Luke Skywalker and the shattering of his fledgling Jedi following, the cosmic Force has lain dormant, seemingly quieted to those able to sense its presence. The adventures of Rey and Finn on Jakku coincide with a turbulence in the cosmic Force, a sudden ripple indicating the awakening of newfound ability. With the Jedi and their records vanished, few—other than Kylo Ren and his mysterious master— are able to appreciate this occurrence.

Meeting Maz Kanata has a profound effect on Rey. She comes to understand that she is an essential part of a much larger galactic tapestry that is unfurling before her eyes, and that the power of the Force is real.

*Simple hairstyle designed for desert survival*

*Salvaged gauze wrap*

Armored body shell

*Flash-suppressing/ stabilizing muzzle*

### REY'S BLASTER
A gift from Han Solo, Rey's LPA NN-14 blaster pistol has a compact grip to best fit her small hands, but its enlarged power core and reinforced frame means it is sturdy and packs a respectable punch.

*Handle wrapping made from scraps of uniform*

*Blade length adjust*

### SKYWALKER'S LIGHTSABER
Anakin Skywalker constructed this weapon at the start of the Clone Wars, and it was later passed to his son, Luke. Luke lost it in battle on Cloud City, but someone salvaged it from the city's industrial depths.

*Activation matrix*

*Power cell*

**QUARTERSTAFF**

# STARSHIP GRAVEYARD

**A GENERATION AGO**, the last embers of the Galactic Civil War came crashing down onto the dunes of Jakku. The secluded planet, far on the fringes of the Western Reaches, became the final battleground of the Galactic Empire. An intense assault by New Republic warships led to the burning wrecks of vessels from both sides plummeting into Jakku's atmosphere. The battle was ended by news of the peace treaty being signed on distant Coruscant, and the sudden departure of the surviving Imperial warships into the Unknown Regions.

## LUGGABEAST

A cybernetically-enhanced beast of burden found on frontier worlds, luggabeast faces are forever hidden beneath armor plating. Invasive mechanical systems enhance the luggabeast's endurance to well beyond natural levels.

Salvaged speeder bike saddle

Purified air and water recycling tanks

Armored fetlock

Exposed cranial dome reveals reptilian heritage

Catch bottle collects and recycles bodily fluids

Goggles help eliminate desert glare

Mag-pulse grenade

Ionization spear transmits crippling charge

Activation base

Sand-shoes built from rubberized droid treads

## TEEDO

A small, brutish scavenger who roams Jakku's vast Starship Graveyard atop his luggabeast, Teedo is constantly on the prowl for valuable technology. With the zeal of a tyrant, he roams what he believes to be his territory, a patch of desert southwest of Niima Outpost. Using scanners built into the cybernetic cowl that encases his luggabeast, Teedo relentlessly seeks out the energy signatures found in droid power cells.

Teedos have a peculiar sense of identity that does not differentiate between individuals; the name Teedo refers both to a single being and the entire species.

### REY'S SANDBOARD

To help her descend quickly down Jakku's largest dunes, Rey uses a scrap of smooth-hulled Mon Calamari escape pod as a makeshift sled that can carry her and her rucksack.

*Lining is repurposed parachute fabric*

*Fuel port functions as fastening grommet*

### STEELPECKERS

These iron-beaked carrion birds are drawn to the magnetic signature of metal. To better break down their metallic meals, steelpeckers collect vanadium, osmiridium, and corundum in their gizzards.

*Carcasses and guano are a worthwhile commodity*

*Iron-hard talons are sharpened to a deadly point*

**SALVAGED STAR DESTROYER CAPACITOR BEARING**

**DATA FILE**

> Animal life stubbornly persists on Jakku, with transplanted creatures and parasites that survived the starship crashes finding a place in the desert ecology.

> Native life-forms include the little-documented nocturnal sandborer known as the nightwatcher worm.

*Used to pry components from durasteel bulkheads*

**"WESSEX-HEAD" BIT-DRIVER**   **"BLISSEX-HEAD" BIT-DRIVER**   **CARBON CHISEL**   **CHISEL HEAD HAMMER**

Rey keeps a satchel filled with salvage tools that allow her to carry out fine salvage work among the starship wrecks. Unlike many of the brutes that work the Graveyard, she has the keen eye and dexterity required to extract the most valuable pieces of technology.

### THE *RAVAGER*

The huge Super Star Destroyer *Ravager* crashed upside down. Its rusting halls have a sinister reputation, even among hardened scavengers.

# WRECKED SHIPS

Jakku was once home to a secret Imperial research facility, and was the last rallying point of the Imperial fleet. Entering the atmosphere to tighten its cordon, the Empire fought determinedly to keep the New Republic from capturing the base. In its defense, doomed Imperial vessels used tractor beams to drag New Republic warships into the planet's surface. The retreating Imperials destroyed the base before disappearing into the Unknown Regions.

*Remains of the Star Destroyer* Inflictor

*Conning tower has become home to squatters*

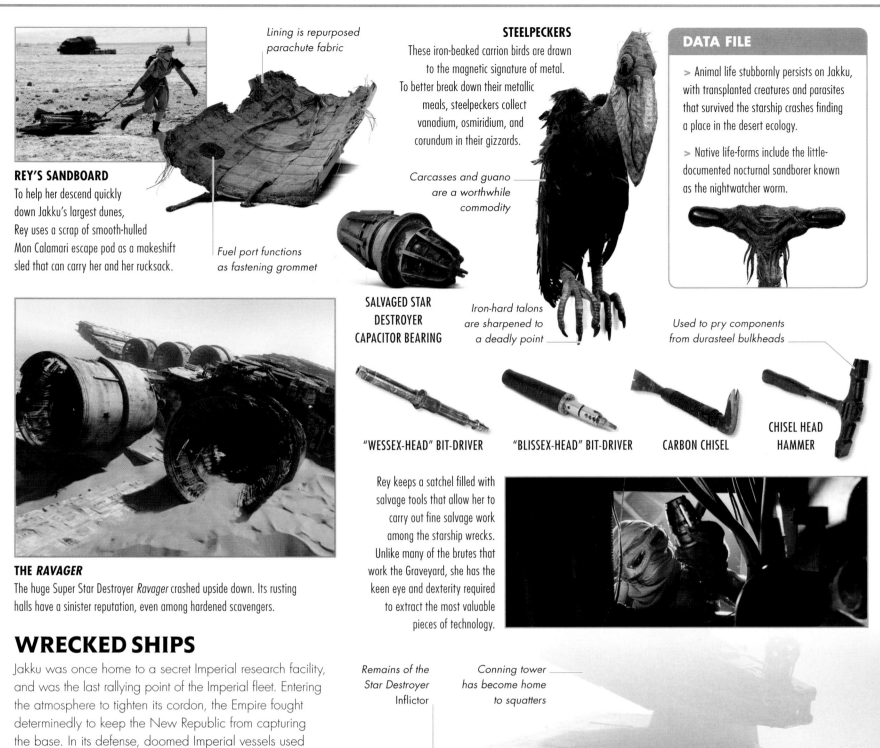

# NIIMA OUTPOST

**SINCE THE WAR** that littered Jakku's landscape with debris, the planet has become a treasure trove for prospectors and scavengers of wildly varying means and fortunes. Niima Outpost, a crumbling settlement of rickety landing bays, dusty salvage yards, and the type of shady businesses that parasitically flourish around the desperate, is the closest thing Jakku has to a city. Interstellar travelers looking to find riches or lose pursuers keep a steady trickle of traffic coming to and from the outpost.

## NIIMA ORIGINS

After the Battle of Jakku, opportunists pounced to recover valuable metal, weapons, and scraps of technology from the scattered crash sites. The first enterprising scoundrel that sought to organize the collection efforts was Niima the Hutt. She was operating far from the borders of Hutt Space— a province of the galaxy embroiled in conflict as the Hutts tried to carve up the deceased crime lord Jabba's territory. Though Niima was later killed by a bounty hunter, the outpost that she established still bears her name.

**EGL-21 "AMPS" POWER DROID**

*Shielded faceplate*

An expert bit of welding might turn unsaleable junk into a profitable find, so "Geetaw" offers his skills in exchange for a power recharge, inert gas canisters, filler metals, or a good joke.

*Plasma arc welder torch*

**GTAW-74 WELDER DROID**

### HAPPABORE

Found on several worlds, perhaps as a result of some forgotten colonial effort, the happabore is a strong, hardy creature with tough skin, an enormous snout, and remarkable obedience.

*Traditional Kyuzo war helmet*

*Face wrapped to prevent sunburn*

*Sensor pack with extensible antenna*

*Salvaged metal hammered into armor*

*Breathable tsu-seed linen tunic*

### CONSTABLE ZUVIO

Providing a semblance of law and order in Niima Outpost is Constable Zuvio, leader of a local militia that includes two of his fellow Kyuzo warriors. Zuvio has a strong sense of justice and cannot be bribed.

# NIIMA RESIDENTS

New arrivals on Jakku are inevitably drawn to Niima Outpost as it is the only navigational beacon on the planet. Salvage forms the backbone of Niima's economy, but other services have sprung up to take advantage of newcomers. Black market trading, guns-for-hire, and other disreputable activities thrive on a planet with minimal laws.

Salvaged metal vibro-halberd

Cage contains Bobbajo's pet worrt

Hose supplies processed atmosphere

Sneep

Mechanical load-lifter replacement arms

## SARCO PLANK
One-time scavenger, bounty hunter, and tomb raider, Sarco Plank is an aging Melitto who has made a multitude of enemies in his checkered career. The eyeless being "sees" via supersensitive cilia.

Nutrient and fluid dispenser

## ATHGAR HEECE
A Dybrinthe bounty hunter used to operating in higher atmospheric pressures and temperatures, Heece actually finds Jakku quite pleasant.

## BOBBAJO
A creaky-jointed Nu-Cosian, Bobbajo's calm demeanor helps settle down the jittery animals he carries on his back to sell at the market.

## "CRUSHER" ROODOWN
Roodown is an unlucky salvager who had his arms cut off by Unkar Plutt's thugs over a misunderstanding. He offers his services as a for-hire strong back.

SoroSuub JSP-14 pistol fitted in tripler

### SARCO'S BLASTER RIFLE

Now an arms dealer, Sarco's business in Niima involves fencing stolen weaponry to travelers looking to brave the Graveyard wastes. To emphasize the quality of his wares, Sarco brandishes an exotic Trandoshan tripler, an attachment that increases the firepower of any compatible blaster weapon.

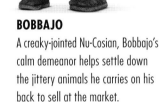

"JAKKU NIGHT SPECIAL" BLASTER RIFLE

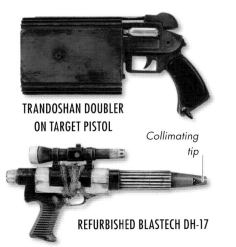

## TRANDOSHAN DOUBLER ON TARGET PISTOL

Collimating tip

### REFURBISHED BLASTECH DH-17

There are very few permanent structures on Jakku. The marketplace, even though a fixture of Niima Outpost, consists mostly of cargo containers and temporary awnings. There is little in the way of accommodations, and most travelers opt to sleep aboard their starships.

37

# UNKAR PLUTT

**A HARSH DESERT PLANET** is the last place one would expect to find an alien of aquatic origins, but Unkar Plutt goes where profit, not nature, dictates. Removed from his saltwater surroundings, Unkar's Crolute body sags unsettlingly on his frame, giving him the appearance of a melted blobfish. This only adds to his unappealing demeanor as the junk boss of Jakku, who runs a successful business stealing, scavenging, and selling scrap. He doles out slim rations of food in exchange for valuable salvage, and calls upon goons and henchmen to ensure he gets the best deals.

*Buoyant, gelatinous body tissue*

*Leather cap with electroloupe*

*Sour demeanor*

**VEG-MEAT**

**POLYSTARCH**

From behind a caged window within his stall, Unkar casts a discerning eye over fresh salvage delivered by Rey. Impressed, he grants her a quarter portion of rations.

Unkar's workspace is a converted cargo crawler. It has been fitted with security monitors to ensure no desperate scavengers attempt to steal any of his provisions.

*Long-range antenna, as Jakku lacks a communications grid*

*Audio grid and tuning dial*

**UNKAR'S COMLINK**

## JUNKYARD BOSS

Unkar's trading stall stands at the center of one of the few semi-permanent structures within Niima Outpost, an awning-roofed blockhouse the locals call the "Concession Stand." Unkar has a monopoly on food supplies, and is the principal source of nourishment for scavengers who work the junkfields. In exchange for valuable salvage that he can sell for real credits, Unkar doles out survival rations. He sells the salvage to spacers on Jakku, or on nearby worlds like Ponemah Terminal and Ogem.

*Apron made from salvaged hull plates*

**Radiation-proof head wrappings**

## UNKAR'S THUGS

Unkar takes his complete control over survival rations on Jakku seriously, and sets aside some of his wealth to pay for a gang of dim-witted henchmen. These lackeys keep an eye out for unauthorized barter or off-world food.

Unkar maintains a number of cleaning stations at Niima Outpost, where he makes supplies available to restore salvage into more presentable condition. The cost of renting a table is deducted from the final trading price.

**Glare-blocking goggles**

## ANONYMOUS MUSCLE

The thugs under Unkar's employ keep their faces wrapped to conceal their identities, to avoid reprisals during their "off-hours." They are too dim-witted to realize that their body language, voices, and belligerent attitudes are easy to identify.

**Vibro-shiv concealed within boot**

**Salvaged from a fuel injector within a Star Destroyer positional thruster**

**Quadanium sheath**

**MEDIUM INVERTER**

**CATALYST REACTANT CRADLE**

**Gloves with padded knuckles**

**Easily concealable**

**All serial numbers removed**

Rey's spirited independence has put her at odds with Unkar in the past, though Plutt still considers her one of his best scroungers. She can hold her own against thugs far more physically imposing than herself.

**Plastoid-tipped boots**

**SNUB-BLASTER**

# GENERAL HUX

**A YOUNG, RUTHLESS OFFICER** in the First Order, General Hux has complete confidence in his troops, training methods, and weaponry. He has grown up celebrating his Imperial heritage—his father was a highly placed official in the Imperial Academy of old—and Hux feels it is a matter of destiny that he be given a chance to sit on the throne that rules the galaxy. Hux's experiences in warfare are entirely theoretical. Few would question the thoroughness or complexity of his simulations, but Kylo Ren in particular has little respect for Hux as a warrior.

Pallor from time spent indoors

Charcoal gray general's uniform

Formal parade stance

Polished officer's buckle

Traditional flared-hip breeches

Insulated boots

A tense competitiveness exists between Kylo Ren and Hux, as both vie for the attention and approval of the First Order's mysterious commander, Supreme Leader Snoke.

## DATA FILE

> A man of science and technology, Hux has little understanding of or patience for the mystical side of the First Order that Kylo Ren represents.

> Hux's rank of general extends beyond the control of armies; he is the commander of the Starkiller operation, and able to order its use—pending Snoke's approval.

Hux continues to use the stormtrooper training regimen pioneered by his father, based on ideas the elder Hux hatched as an Academy commandant. Hux has total confidence in his father's idea that stormtroopers trained through vivid simulations make the most loyal soldiers.

## IMPERIOUS DESTINY

Hux was a child when the Empire surrendered to the New Republic with the signing of the Galactic Concordance. His father fled the Academy on Arkanis, and was one of the Imperials to make the exodus into the Unknown Regions, which the Empire had secretly been exploring. Hux grew up hearing legends of great Imperials, and how the Empire saved the galaxy from the violence of the Clone Wars. The young Hux firmly believed the galaxy needed to be saved from itself, as the New Republic was too weak to prevent the inevitable chaos.

## RANK INSIGNIA

The First Order uses a commemorative rank insignia system, consisting of armbands bearing the names of famous units and heroes of the Galactic Civil War.

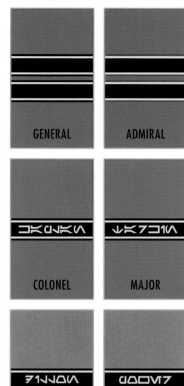

GENERAL

ADMIRAL

COLONEL

MAJOR

CAPTAIN

LIEUTENANT

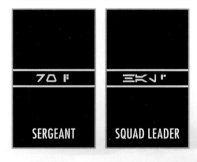

SERGEANT

SQUAD LEADER

When chaos erupts in the hangar bay of the *Finalizer*, Hux oversees the attempts to capture the wayward TIE fighter that has caused the disruption.

GENERAL'S COMMAND CAP

Heat dispersing barrel head

Power cell

### HUX'S BLASTER

The officer's edition of the standard stormtrooper sidearm is cast in dark plasteel as opposed to the white body of the infantry version.

Trigger is coded to Hux's fingerprint

Lasing chamber access pins

Crested command cap

Gaberwool officer's greatcoat

First Order insignia

## WAR LEADER

When Hux stands upon the Starkiller superweapon, he can feel its destructive power coursing through the world. He knows it will signal the end of the illegitimate New Republic and cause the galaxy to bow to the power of the First Order. To Hux, the future of warfare is now—a war that can be won with a single shot.

Hux has always believed that appearances are vital for maintaining discipline, and wears a parade uniform designed to broadcast his authority as general.

Ranks of TIE fighters

Base defense walker

# FINALIZER CREW

**THE GALACTIC CONCORDANCE** prevented the First Order from accessing the scattered Academies that had filled out the ranks of the Imperial Navy. Instead, the surviving Imperials created new Academies far from the prying eyes of the New Republic, situating them aboard Star Destroyers built in hidden shipyards on the far side of the galaxy. The young fleet officers produced by these shipboard schools often spend their entire lives aboard Star Destroyers, and many think of these giant warships as their homes.

**Crested command cap**

## LIEUTENANT MITAKA

Dopheld Mitaka graduated at the top of his Academy class, earning a prestigious placement aboard the *Finalizer*. He wears a commemorative armband that bears the name of a notable admiral of the Old Empire.

*Rank cylinders*

*Insulated helmet with integrated data displays*

*Flame-resistant duty uniform*

## FIRST ORDER FLEET

Though too small to rival the navy of the Galactic Empire at its height, the First Order fleet is nonetheless a formidable concentration of spaceborne destructive power. The New Republic, with what First Order admirals mock as typical shortsightedness, was so thorough in its galactic disarmament that the First Order's secret fleet of Star Destroyers now stands almost unchallenged.

*Lieutenant armband*

*Concealed tool pouches*

Lieutenant Mitaka's impressive academic career proves to be inadequate when faced with the fierce temper of Kylo Ren.

## FLEET ENGINEER

Whether maintaining the power or weapon systems of the *Finalizer,* or operating its powerful turbolaser, tractor beam, or missile emplacements, engineers carry out their orders with precision.

With its immense hangar space, each *Resurgent*-class Star Destroyer carries with it the operational challenges of a bustling spaceport.

*Stiff boots help in maintaining posture*

# BRIDGE PERSONNEL

First Order starship crews work closely together to ensure the smooth operation of their massive vessels. Ever-mobile and immensely complex, Star Destroyers require constant attention from their personnel. As a result, each standard day is divided into six four-hour-long shifts, divided among three crew sections. Each section fosters a strong sense of unity and team identity.

The bridges of *Resurgent*-class Star Destroyers are much better protected than the exposed conning towers of old Imperial warships. The sunken work stations, a design that dates back to the Clone Wars-era Jedi cruisers, continue to be the preferred layout for architecturally denoting command hierarchy.

### BRIDGE SCREENS
Simplified bridge displays with limited colors allow for the rapid dissemination of complicated data.

## DATA FILE

> Access to command systems and certain areas of First Order vessels and installations is governed by coded rank cylinders worn by officers.

> The Resistance has limited intelligence of the First Order fleet, and many fear that the *Resurgent*-class is not the largest of the new Star Destroyer designs.

Command order tray (retracted)

Biological systems monitoring sensor

Medical telemetry transmission array

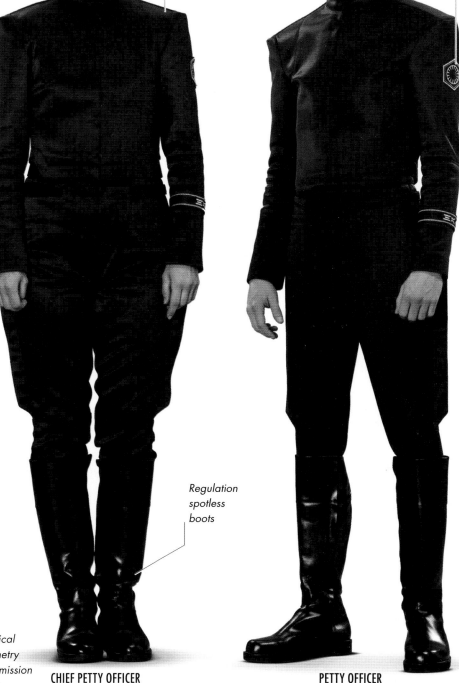

Intercom headset

Lighter fabric duty uniform

First Order insignia

Regulation spotless boots

**CHIEF PETTY OFFICER UNAMO**

**PETTY OFFICER THANISSON**

### INTERROGATION DROID
Developed in violation of strict New Republic laws prohibiting torture, the new generation IT-000 is a corruption of medical droid tech.

### MOUSE DROID
A tireless mainstay from the days of the Old Republic, the skittish Rebaxan Columni MSE-series serves as a messenger, repair, and custodial droid aboard First Order starships and installations.

Stormtroopers follow their own chain of command while aboard fleet vessels, with a captain of the guard serving as ultimate authority over the troopers. During alerts, however, troopers will follow orders from any officer regardless of branch of service.

# TIE FIGHTER PILOTS

**ADVANCES IN TECHNOLOGY,** as well as the necessity that comes from no longer being the dominant galactic space force, have greatly benefited the latest generation of TIE fighter pilots. No longer callously treated as simply a line in a military ledger, TIE pilots are now given greater training and support in their missions. Their new generation fighter craft, though strongly resembling the TIEs of old, have a much greater survival rate than that suffered by the TIE pilots of the Galactic Empire.

The rudimentary deflector shields aboard new generation TIE fighters also smooth their passage through atmospheres, granting TIEs greater atmospheric control without needing streamlined modifications to the spaceframe.

## TIE PILOT CORPS

The new generation of TIE fighter pilots undergo rigorous training not unlike the constant and dehumanizing drilling faced by stormtrooper cadets. The pilots begin training at childhood, and most grow up within the corridors of Star Destroyers, becoming intimately familiar with starship operations. The First Order maintains strict standards of reflexes, visual acuity, and hand-eye coordination. Those pilots who fail to measure up are transferred to other roles within the fleet.

*Targeting sensors*

*Complete vac-seal helmet*

*Flight gloves and vambrace armor*

*Dark hull makes spacebound TIEs harder to target with visual scanning*

*Sienar-Jaemus Fleet Systems L-s9.6 laser cannon*

### TIE FIGHTER
The standard fighter craft of the First Order fleet is the TIE/fo, an advanced version of the ubiquitous TIE/ln of the Galactic Civil War.

*Weapon interface*

*Solar collector array wing*

*Left-hand control column*

*Right-hand control column and weapons trigger*

*Ejection harness*

### FLIGHT CONTROLS
A sophisticated Torplex flight computer translates the movements of the pilot's two control columns into micro-adjustments to the twin ion streams that propel the craft.

*Positive gravity pressure boots*

### SF TIE FIGHTER

A more robust edition of the TIE fighter is the Special Forces variant, equipped with a heavy weapons turret (for a tailgunner), limited hyperdrive, and enhanced shield projectors.

Structural bracing

Pre-charged deuterium power cells

Heavy weapons turret

Special Forces unit marking

### DATA FILE

> Standard TIEs have finally been granted deflector shield technology—a profound change in philosophy from the days of the Galactic Empire.

> Aboard First Order Star Destroyers, TIEs are deployed from hangar conveyor mechanisms that carry them up from deeper storage decks.

TIE fighters engage the *Millennium Falcon* over the junk-strewn dunes of Jakku.

Red markings indicate Special Forces status

Ship-linked communications

Targeting node connects to external targeting sensors

Targeting interface projector

SE-44C officer's pistol

Life support gear

"Target acquired"

Padding

Detachable chin unit

Flexible vac-suit

Pilot comlink

**SPECIAL FORCES PILOT HELMET**

Atmosphere hose

A particularly stubborn Special Forces pilot pursues his prey through the inner workings of the derelict Super Star Destroyer *Ravager*.

# SPECIAL FORCES

The distinctive flashes of red that stand out from the all-black armor of some TIE fighters and their pilots are the mark of the Special Forces—elite starfighter pilots answerable directly to the upper command levels of the Starkiller operation. The markings date back to the decorated flight barons of the Old Empire.

# HAN SOLO

**IF ANYTHING** is consistent in Han Solo's life, it is unpredictability. His past exploits are the stuff of legends—he has been the famed smuggler who smashed the record for the Kessel Run; the onetime captain of the *Millennium Falcon*; the death-marked fugitive who outran Boba Fett and outlived the ire of Jabba the Hutt; and the scoundrel who won the heart of the last princess of Alderaan and became a hero of the Rebellion. Transition to a time of peace has not been easy for Han, who never expected an early or tranquil retirement. As the pendulum of fate once more swings the galaxy into war, he once again finds himself in the center of the chaos.

*Former brown hair now entirely gray*

*Nerf-leather jacket*

*Still a fast draw*

## OLD HABITS

After the Galactic Civil War, Han Solo's life took unexpected turns as he became husband to an influential New Republic politician, a family man, and—for a time—a successful racing pilot. But the peace of this life was not to last, and after a profound tragedy upended what had become normal for the Corellian, Solo returned to his old life as a tramp freighter captain, smuggler, and freelance law bender. Chewbacca returned to Solo's side, and although much had changed, in many ways it was like the old days.

*Trigger*

**DETONATOR**

Han and Chewie are surprised to find stowaways aboard the *Millennium Falcon*, but quickly realize that the inexperienced youngsters do not pose a threat.

**HAN'S WELDING GOGGLES**

*Detachable macroscope*

**HAN'S HEAVY BLASTER PISTOL**

Han continues to favor the BlasTech DL-44 design he has carried since before the Galactic Civil War, even though newer models have come and gone.

*Power cell*

*Low-power pulse warning*

*Captain's pants devoid of markings*

> Solo never considered himself sentimental as a young man, but now finds himself treasuring relics of when he was in his prime.

> The younger Solo once scoffed at any mention of the Force, but now says without reservation that its power is real.

A brief visit to Takodana and the sanctuary of Maz Kanata's pirate den is suddenly interrupted by an unmistakable show of force by the First Order.

# FOR THE RESISTANCE

Though Solo tries to remain apolitical he cannot abandon his conscience when it becomes apparent that the Resistance needs him. For Han, it is less about lofty ideals of freedom and democracy than it is to answer impassioned pleas for help from Rey, Finn, and ultimately, Leia Organa. Solo suits up for trouble and charges into danger, plunging into the very heart of the First Order, in an attempt to make a difference in as foolhardy and reckless a way as possible: a classic Han Solo gambit.

Cargo containers locked into transport grid

Cold weather gear

Bridge

Propulsion module

Docking bay door

Over the years, the *Falcon* has switched hands from Lando Calrissian to Solo, from Solo to Ducain, from Ducain to the Irving Boys, from the Irving Boys to Unkar Plutt, from Unkar Plutt to Rey, and back to Solo.

# SHIPS OF FORTUNE

As easily as the *Millennium Falcon* fell into Solo's life after a heated game of sabacc, so it was destined to abandon him after a change in fate. Solo made do with other ships at his disposal, eventually settling on an enormous bulk freighter named the *Eravana*, which he uses to haul massive shipments of legally questionable cargo. The ship is largely automated, meaning Solo and Chewbacca can handle most of the work, but on particularly dangerous or profitable hauls he hires additional hands.

Cooling vent

**SCOUNDREL'S LUCK**
Solo has kept the golden pair of dice that he used in the "Corellian Spike" game of sabacc in which he won the *Millennium Falcon* from Lando Calrissian.

Replacement sensor dish

Insulated boots

Cockpit

# CHEWBACCA

**FAITHFUL FIRST MATE** and copilot Chewbacca has loyally stood by his captain's side through the twisting fortunes of a galaxy in turmoil. Devoted to Solo no matter what ship the Corellian pilot happens to be flying, Chewie serves as a mechanical mastermind, keeping ships operational after Solo's harebrained maneuvers push them to their limit. As a long-lived Wookiee, the decades that Chewie has spent at Solo's side are scant payment of the life debt that Chewie feels he owes Solo. The two continue to be inseparable friends.

## WOUNDED WARRIOR

A run-in with competing gangs over a matter of credits owed results in Chewbacca suffering a blaster wound. Though the wound is suitably field-dressed, it requires a closer inspection from a medical professional. Doctor Kalonia of the Resistance applies her skilled touch to the injured Wookiee.

### MEDICAL KIT
Kalonia's field kit is well equipped to handle blaster burns, with antiseptic field generators, bacta bulbs, and synthflesh dispensers within easy reach.

*Stowed gear in cushioned case*

*Handheld healing field generator*

### TOOL KIT
Despite the *Falcon's* ramshackle appearance, Chewbacca is surprisingly particular when it comes to the storage of his tools. He often wishes Han was the same.

Soothing words from Kalonia calm the temperamental Chewbacca, who has never been good around doctors. Kalonia's fluency in Shyriiwook makes her a sympathetic ear.

*Macroscope*

*Positive-default alternating polarizer*

*Conductive bowstring*

*Skeletal stalk and butt*

*Woven kshyyy-vine strap*

## BOWCASTER

Chewie's hand-crafted bowcaster is a traditional Wookiee ranged weapon. Colloquially known as a laser crossbow, the weapon uses alternating magnetic polarizers to energize a destructive bolt known as a quarrel. The quarrel emerges from the barrel sheathed in blaster energy, resulting in a particularly explosive impact. The weapon requires Wookiee strength to fire comfortably.

*Negative-default alternating polarizer*

### DATA FILE

> At 234 years old, Chewbacca is still not yet approaching middle age for a Wookiee.

> After the Battle of Endor, Chewbacca helped lead the New Republic effort to liberate Kashyyyk from Imperial rule.

"We're home," declares Han as they recover the *Falcon.* Although Chewie's time aboard the vessel represents a smaller percentage of his life, he is still fond of the ship he invested so much effort into maintaining.

Keen blue eyes

Bandolier cases
contain one
to three bowcaster
quarrels each

Nearly
indestructible
kshyyy-vine weave

Carry-pouch

Pattern of fur
coloration is
unique to each
Wookiee

Climbing claws
(retracted)

Chewbacca is the first Wookiee Finn has ever met. Unable to understand Chewie's language, the young First Order deserter is intimidated.

## PARTNERS IN CRIME

Chewbacca returned to Kashyyyk once it was free from Imperial rule and reconnected with his larger family. Wookiee familial bonds are strong, but occur in a timescale alien to humans with their shorter lifespans. As such, it is relatively easy for Chewbacca to spend decades adventuring in the galaxy, away from his people. When Han Solo returns to a life of smuggling, Chewbacca feels honor-bound to follow his trusted friend down this path and offer what help he can.

### EXPLOSIVES BAG

Chewbacca puts his great strength to good use hauling a rucksack full of pyro denton explosives, during a mission to sabotage the First Order's evil plans.

Ever loyal, Chewbacca accompanies Han Solo on his mission to infiltrate the Starkiller operation. Chewie is Solo's sworn protector and will do all he can to keep him safe.

### BANDOLIER

Chewbacca's bandolier holds ammunition and a carry-pouch containing tools to keep his bowcaster in operational condition.

# GUAVIAN DEATH GANG

**TO BANKROLL HIS HAUL** for King Prana, Han Solo foolishly borrows 50,000 credits from the Guavian Death Gang, a criminal organization formerly based out of the Core Worlds. With the Guavian bosses tired of his excuses and delays, soldiers of the organization shadow Solo's freighter from his departure point on Nantoon. They seek to collect on Solo's overdue loan, and also make clear that a criminal organization with the words "Death Gang" in its name is not to be taken likely. The security soldiers of the Guavian Death Gang wear high-impact armor that makes them stand out among other deadly criminals.

Ruthless gaze

Gorraslug -leather coat

Tostovin Munitions percussive cannon

Armored lining in long coat

Concealed cybernetic leg

Sparadillo armored boots

## BALA-TIK

Guavian frontman Bala-Tik is familiar with Solo's silver tongue, and won't accept another catalog of excuses from the Corellian. Although it would undoubtedly be easy to gun Solo down in cold blood and thus live up to the Death Gang name, Bala-Tik knows Solo to be a valuable source of profitable information. In the past, Bala-Tik has shaken moneymaking leads out of Solo, though his patience with the pilot grows razor-thin.

Bala-Tik speaks with the clipped tones of the Core Worlds, but with a harsher edge.

Targeting sight somewhat unnecessary, given weapon's blast radius

Reinforced kinetic channeler

Recoil counterweight calibrator

### PERCUSSIVE CANNON

Bala-Tik and the rest of the Guavians carry the latest in black market technology, such as massive percussive cannons that fire particularly explosive blaster bolts.

### DATA FILE

> Following the collapse of the Galactic Empire and the transfer of the capital off of Coruscant, the Core World criminal underworld underwent massive changes.

> The Guavians were displaced and reformed in the Inner Rim and Colonies regions.

### MASKS

Guavian security soldiers communicate via high frequency data streams transmitted from the central disk in their faceplates. They are otherwise expressionless, giving them an even greater air of menace.

### DEADLY WEAPONRY

The Guavians have contacts throughout the armament industry and pay a steep price for the latest weapon prototypes to go "missing" and end up in their hands.

*Fore sight*

*Serial numbers completely obliterated*

*"Sawed-off" percussive cannon*

*Recoil compensator*

*Stabilizing grip*

*Tostovin Munitions micro-grenade launcher*

*Magazine drum*

*Central sensor and broadcasting dish*

*Arterial chemical shunt*

*Ablative gorget armor*

## SECURITY SOLDIERS

The Guavian Death Gang's red-armored foot soldiers are faceless killers who have sworn loyalty in exchange for cybernetic augmentation. A mechanical reservoir pump acts as a second heart, injecting a secret concoction of chemicals directly into the bloodstream, boosting a Guavian soldier's speed and aggression to deadly levels. Everything about them is inhuman and highly illegal.

*Flexible armor shin guard*

*Reactant emitter barrels*

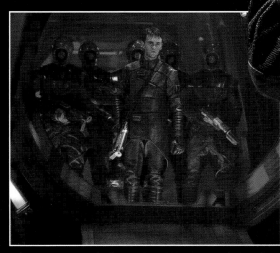

Bala-Tik is wary enough of Han Solo and Chewbacca to bring with him an armored contingent of security soldiers. He suspects Solo will be crazy enough to start a gunfight near an airlock.

*Segmented gauntlets*

*Utility belt*

# KANJIKLUB

**AN OUTER RIM GANG** of ruffians that often comes into the conflict with the Guavian Death Gang, Kanjiklub has found common ground with their rivals in the form of a mutual hatred of Han Solo. The sly Corellian smuggler has borrowed money from both outfits to complete his risky cargo haul, and neither organization cares for Solo taking such risks with their capital. Added to that, Solo has twice left Kanjiklub empty-handed after failures to deliver cargo.

## DATA FILE

> Kanjiklub hails from Nar Kanji, a Hutt colony world left in disarray following a gang war within the Hutt cartels.

> Formerly subjugated by the Hutts, the human colonists of Nar Kanji overthrew their overlords and struck out on their own.

*Unkempt, feral appearance*

*Plastoid blast jerkin*

*Narglatch tusk vibro-spike*

**TASU LEECH'S "HUTTSPLITTER" BLASTER RIFLE**

*Hand-assembled blaster body*

*Gundark bone grip*

## TASU LEECH

Tasu Leech is the nominal leader of the scruffy Kanjiklub gang. Unlike their more organized and polished Guavian rivals, Kanjiklub resembles an unruly group of streetfighters and weapon-wielding thugs who dabble in extortion, piracy, and starship theft. Leech is not one for elaborate plans and rarely thinks beyond the next raid. Traditional to his frontier roots, he refuses to speak a word of Basic, deeming it a "soft language for soft people," though he can understand it well enough.

*Bell-mouthed blaster increases bolt spread*

**DONDERBUS BLASTER**

*Flexorcord-fastened assembly*

*Oversized amplifiers increase blaster bolt charge within barrel*

*Kintan strider ulna handle*

*Lightweight armor does not impede agility*

In accordance with Kanjiklub tradition, the leader of the gang may be challenged to combat by his underlings at any time. Tasu Leech has defeated many would-be usurpers to his command.

## KANJIKLUB MEMBERS

During their long enslavement by the Hutts, the human colonists of Nar Kanji developed fighting styles that incorporated improvised weaponry, both melee and ranged. The modern Kanjiklubbers celebrate the ingenuity that kept their ancestors alive, and typically equip themselves with intimidating patchwork armor, jury-rigged rifles, blades, and clubs.

Flame-retardant uniform

Tibanna-jacked boiler rifle

Braced firing stance for intense recoil

**VOLZANG LI-THRULL**

The raucous nature of Kanjiklub and the constant vying for dominance within the ranks means the ragtag group rarely operates well as a team, unless Tasu Leech is directly in command.

Pit-fighting injuries

Roggwart-bone rifle butt

Cybernetic leg rigged for fierce kicks

**CROKIND SHAND**

Zygerrian-style faux crests

Homemade explosive cylinders

Insulated palm sparring gloves

Scope largely for show on short-range weapon

Extended recoil-absorbing stalk

**LI-THRULL'S BOILER RIFLE**

Spin-sealed Tibanna bottle

External accelerator barrel cage

**QIN-FEE'S "WASP" BLASTER RIFLE**

Pump action gas compression

Reinforced-galven circuit barrel

**SHAND'S HEAVY BORE RIFLE**

## RAZOO QIN-FEE

A lieutenant to Tasu Leech, Razoo Qin-Fee was banned from the underworld Zygerrian fighting circuit for suspected cheating—a remarkable feat in a sport that has no rules. A pyromaniac and tech expert, Razoo maintains the hodgepodge weaponry and explosives favored by the wild Kanjiklubbers, frequently upgrading and modifying their deadly tools of the trade to exacting and sinister specifications.

# GENERAL ORGANA

Leia has shed any symbols of royalty unless tradition demands it

**IT IS NO SMALL IRONY** that the woman who embodied the ideals of peace and freedom for one generation was branded a militant fearmonger by the next. Many thought Leia Organa was unreasonably suspicious of the peace process that defanged the Galactic Empire. She argued that the New Republic was not doing enough to secure the safety of its citizens, and she was estranged from the Senate for her refusal to let the ghosts of the last war stay dead. Leia's words of warning regarding the First Order's mobilization for war prove tragically prophetic.

Rank badges are red for army personnel, and blue for navy

Snub-nose collimating barrel tip

Rank-free vest

Resistance uniform

Ammunition power cell

GENERAL/ADMIRAL

COLONEL

COMMANDER

MAJOR

CAPTAIN

LIEUTENANT

### LEIA'S BLASTER
Leia's preference has always been for compact hand weapons. The Eirriss Ryloth Defense Tech Glie-44 is a Resistance mainstay.

On the smoking battlefield of Takodana, Leia encounters Han Solo in an awkward reunion. Their complicated feelings must be put aside to focus on the graver matters at hand.

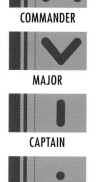

In the heart of the D'Qar base command center, Leia Organa keeps track of Resistance operations. Never far from her side are Admiral Statura, whom she relies upon for advice and perspective, and the protocol droid C-3PO.

## RESISTANCE LEADER

Leia Organa's words of warning about the suspicious activities of the First Order far from the eyes of the Republic fall on deaf ears. Many in the Senate are content with the peace that has been won, regardless of the increasing cold war tensions between Republic and First Order. They brand Leia as an alarmist at best, a warmonger at worst. Not even Leia's royal status as the last princess of Alderaan commands much authority, as such titles now hold little sway in a Republic determined to uphold the tenets of democracy.

*BlasTech EL-16HFE blaster rifle*

*Troop cabin with rack-suspended seats*

## RESISTANCE TRANSPORT

The Resistance's transports were cobbled together from parts left over from previous wars, creating an unusual-looking vessel for conveying troops to the battlefield.

*R-9X heavy laser cannon*

*Multi-layered armored hatch*

*Armored B-wing Mark 2 cockpit module*

# RESISTANCE INFANTRY

The Resistance is so undermanned that nearly all of its personnel do double duty (or more), serving as ground troops. Scanner technicians, droid programers, starship mechanics—all are willing to don a combat helmet and pick up a blaster rifle to do battle with the First Order should circumstances call for it.

*Visor flips down to protect face during combat*

**RESISTANCE COMBAT HELMET**

*New jacket—though Leia didn't notice*

Nearly everyone in the Resistance command center on D'Qar was personally recruited by Leia Organa, convinced by her plea to act where the Republic could or would not. Leia knows everyone under her command by name, a fact not taken for granted by her crew.

# HAN AND LEIA

Tumultuous would be a fitting word to describe the relationship between Han Solo and Leia Organa. In their younger days, when faced with the backdrop of war, their opposite natures and impulsive drives led them to romance. Their feelings have stood the test of time, even though the dynamics of their relationship have been forced to change, adapting in the face of external conflicts and personal tragedy. The two will always share a love that comes from knowing someone so completely.

Leia is grateful for Finn's help, and does not hold his past as a First Order stormtrooper against him. She knows full well how fate and hardship may suddenly cause a hero to emerge from the most unlikely places.

**THE UPPER LEVELS** of the Resistance consist primarily of veterans of the Galactic Civil War who have remained loyal to Princess Leia Organa. Many of the New Republic politicians who rebuilt the Senate thought the best way to preserve peace was to disband the galactic-scale military forces that had become the norm since the Clone Wars. This left many skilled veterans without commands. When Leia began organizing a Resistance to stand watch against the militarized rise of the First Order, these old rebels were ready for the fight.

*Premature graying, common in the Resistance*

### MAJOR BRANCE

A communications officer who keeps General Organa up to date with the latest intelligence on First Order operations, Brance grows weary of always imparting bad news.

*Resistance command officer's uniform*

*Repurposed Rebel Alliance crest*

*Resistance operations tunic*

*Admiral's rank badge*

The command staff of the Resistance base on D'Qar gets a sobering briefing regarding the destructive capabilities of the First Order's Starkiller weapon.

Statura's knack for quickly assessing a situation makes him one of Leia's most trusted officers.

### ADMIRAL STATURA

Statura was only a teenager when the war against the Empire ended, but he had already faced combat in trying to liberate his homeworld of Garel. He is pragmatic and technically minded, and was pursuing a career in applied sciences when General Organa recruited him as commander of ship procurement and logistics in the Resistance.

*Skin faded with age*

### DOCTOR KALONIA

Kalonia's sympathetic bedside manner and good humor is warm enough to offer even the most hardened soldier comfort.

*Medical services armband*

*Eyes evolved for use both underwater and in atmospheres*

*Holds army rank of major*

### MAJOR EMATT

A veteran of the Rebel Alliance dating back to the Battle of Yavin, Ematt is a seasoned soldier who is well traveled across the galaxy.

*Major rank badge*

*Boots emphasize comfort for long hours standing*

*Simple belt clasp*

Resistance personnel have great respect for Admiral Ackbar as one of the few remaining commanders to have faced the terrible might of the Empire at its height.

# ADMIRAL ACKBAR

Ackbar brings to the Resistance nearly six decades of combat experience. He defended the oceans of his planet in the Clone Wars, and brought the rebels much needed warships when he led his people into the Alliance. Following the decisive victory at the Battle of Endor, Ackbar was instrumental in the final defeat of the Empire at Jakku. He was coaxed out of peaceful retirement on Mon Cala by the insistence of General Leia Organa.

**THE YOUNGEST AND BRIGHTEST** of the Resistance military fill out the ranks of its starfighter forces. The Resistance sources these pilots from worlds liberated by the New Republic from the worst of the Empire's oppression. Recruited from the local planetary defense forces, and prepared to fight for the ideals of the former Rebellion, these pilots prove to be a loyal, spirited lot, eager to bring the battle to the First Order. They form a close-knit bond within their squadrons, and continue to fly the seal of the Rebellion made famous in the Galactic Civil War.

FreiTek life support unit

## SNAP WEXLEY

Snap hails from Akiva, an Outer Rim world that was an Imperial base until it was liberated by the New Republic. He is the son of a Rebel Alliance Y-wing pilot who flew at the Battle of Endor. Now a captain in the Resistance, Snap is the best recon flier in the force, with a keen eye for trouble and the piloting skill to evade it.

Detachable holster

Padded flight gauntlets

Signal flares

Positive grip soles

Streamlined S-foil configuration

Astromech socket

Flight computer

Long-range laser cannon

Advanced split-engine design

## T–70 X–WING

The modern X-wing starfighter continues to use many of the design features of the venerable T-65. Improvements include refined engines and a variable-configuration droid socket that supports a wider variety of astromech types. The T-70 also has modular secondary weapon pods, allowing the proton torpedo launchers to be swapped out for different ordnance or even additional laser cannons. This has increased the X-wing's versatility as a space superiority fighter.

Insulated flight helmet

Older Cobalt Squadron logo

Tierfon Yellow Aces sigil

Older Coalstreak Squadron stripes

**ELLO ASTY'S HELMET**

**JESS PAVA'S HELMET**

**NIEN NUNB'S HELMET**

## SQUADRONS

The Resistance base on D'Qar maintains two primary X-wing squadrons, code-named Red and Blue. Blue Squadron is the primary line of defense for the base, with Red Squadron flying as support. Commander Poe Dameron leads both squadrons, under the call sign Black Leader—not as an indication of a separate squadron, but to denote his specialized fighter, *Black One*.

Combat missions typically break the squadron into paired fighter elements, consisting of a lead and a wingman.

Abednedish lettering

Modified native Sullustan gear

Inflatable flight vest

Glie-44 blaster pistol

The intuitive controls of the X-wing remain largely unchanged, meaning inexperienced bush pilots can quickly and confidently take up the stick.

Spacer's flight belt

Ejection harness

**SIGNAL FLARES IN BANDOLIER**

**ELLO ASTY**

Guidenhauser flight harness

"Interstellar orange" color

### DATA FILE

> The current generation of fighter pilots venerate the past with maneuvers named for heroes of the Galactic Civil War. The Skywalker Swoop, the Antilles Intercept, and the Porkins Belly Run are all training basics for Resistance pilots.

**NIEN NUNB**

**JESS PAVA**

# RESISTANCE GROUND CREW

**THE RESISTANCE MAKES DO** with a small arsenal of upgraded starfighters, mostly of the X-wing variety. To keep these ships in fighting shape, the Resistance relies on tireless ground crews who recognize the enormous value these fighters contribute to the war effort. The Resistance has little in the way of capital ships, since Republic demilitarization efforts have made them difficult to obtain. As such, the fighters have to do the bulk of the work to defend worlds targeted by the First Order for expansion and colonization.

Comlink headset

Sound-dampening work helmet

Communications headset

GLD (Ground Logistics Division) controller's coat

Amphibian characteristics

Inventory datapad

Static discharge prevention coveralls

Duty uniform pants

**GOSS TOOWERS**

**BOLLIE PRINDEL**

### ELECTROBINOCULARS
Ground crew spotters monitor the arrival and departure of starship traffic with simple yet reliable instruments.

Controller Dand is a stickler for detail, and does not tolerate anyone operating out of protocol.

**VOBER DAND**

## COMMAND CENTER

The Resistance base on D'Qar was originally scouted as a potential Rebel base by Corona Squadron during the Galactic Civil War. The Rebel Alliance established a short-lived outpost there just prior to the mop-up operations against the retreating Imperial forces. When the resource-strapped Resistance began operations, it relied on old Rebellion-era bases as starting points.

# RESISTANCE DROIDS

Power droids, comms droids, astromechs, and loading droids all play a vital role in keeping the Resistance fighting. With only periodic recharge and maintenance breaks, they diligently work around the chrono to keep equipment operative or to monitor communications and sensor data. Continuing the tradition established by the Rebel Alliance, Resistance droids are granted independence and responsibility and are seen as more than just machines.

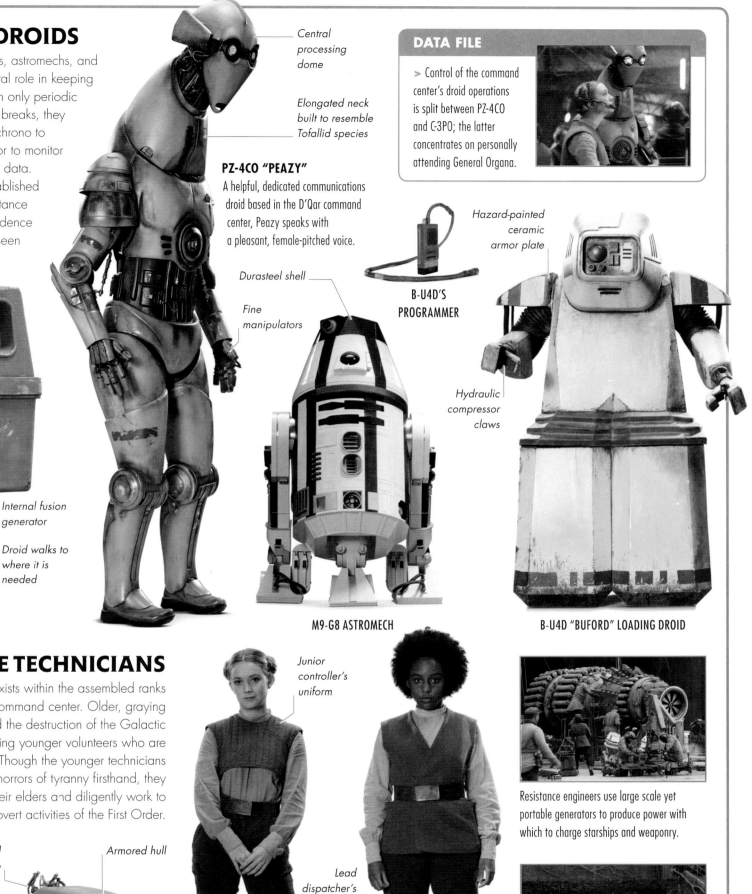

Central processing dome

Elongated neck built to resemble Tofallid species

## PZ-4CO "PEAZY"

A helpful, dedicated communications droid based in the D'Qar command center, Peazy speaks with a pleasant, female-pitched voice.

Durasteel shell

Fine manipulators

B-U4D'S PROGRAMMER

Hazard-painted ceramic armor plate

Hydraulic compressor claws

**DATA FILE**

> Control of the command center's droid operations is split between PZ-4CO and C-3PO; the latter concentrates on personally attending General Organa.

Internal fusion generator

Droid walks to where it is needed

**4B-EG-6**
**GNK-SERIES POWER DROID**

**M9-G8 ASTROMECH**

**B-U4D "BUFORD" LOADING DROID**

# RESISTANCE TECHNICIANS

A generational divide exists within the assembled ranks of the Resistance command center. Older, graying officers who witnessed the destruction of the Galactic Empire lead, inspiring younger volunteers who are barely in their twenties. Though the younger technicians have not witnessed the horrors of tyranny firsthand, they believe the words of their elders and diligently work to track and stop the covert activities of the First Order.

Junior controller's uniform

Lead dispatcher's uniform

Resistance engineers use large scale yet portable generators to produce power with which to charge starships and weaponry.

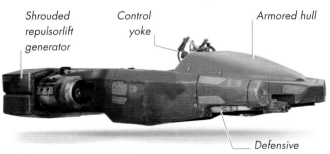

Shrouded repulsorlift generator

Control yoke

Armored hull

Defensive laser cannons

**RESISTANCE BASE SPEEDER**

A battered Gian-211 patrol speeder serves as an example of the Resistance philosophy of using every asset possible. Technicians keep the antiquated repulsorlifts on the transport and recon vehicle working.

**KAYDEL KO**

**PAMICH NERRO**

The D'Qar Resistance base lies underneath foliage-covered mounds. A landing strip assists pilots in avoiding the towering vegetation.

# C-3PO

**A FUSSY PROTOCOL DROID** with decades of continuous functioning, C-3PO serves General Organa to the best of his programed ability. Though he has never felt comfortable in wartime, C-3PO has begrudgingly accepted that a war room will be his base of operations for most of his mechanical lifetime. C-3PO has seen a promotion in his duties since the Rebellion; in addition to his responsibilities as translator, he is also in charge of the movement's pool of spy droids distributed across the galaxy.

C-3PO has served the Organa household since Leia was born. Leia can't help but think of him as a fixture in her life.

## SPYMASTER

All Resistance droids can maintain a communication link to one another via a special protocol partially engineered by C-3PO. With a great knowledge of droid languages from across the galaxy, C-3PO manages the influx of information that comes from droids in the field. He laments that he neglected to activate the tracking protocol on BB-8 prior to its latest mission.

*Intermotor actuating coupler*

During stressful times in the Resistance command center, C-3PO deeply wishes that R2-D2 was operating at full capacity again.

*Logic function computer*

*Audio sensor*

*Salvaged arm*

*Back plate covering mechacarpal assembly*

# R2-D2

AN ASTROMECH DROID that first saw action during the twilight of the Republic, R2-D2 is finally beginning to show his age as newer and more advanced models become the norm for starship support duty. For several years now, R2-D2 has not been operating at peak capacity. His celebrated role in the Rebellion has afforded him semi-retirement rather than the standard recycling the resource-strapped Resistance would normally employ.

Though R2-D2 remains unresponsive, C-3PO still regularly talks to him, fusses over him, and even finds ways to argue with him.

R2-D2 was a constant companion to Luke Skywalker during his journeys across the galaxy following the Battle of Endor, and was witness to triumph and tragedy.

*Acoustic signaler*

*Primary photoreceptor*

## STANDBY MODE

As R2-D2 recuperates in his self-imposed low power mode, his diagnostic systems are attempting to organize the vast trove of information in his databanks from over seven decades of uninterrupted operation. The defragmenting of millions of exanodes within his memory is causing R2-D2 to "dream" many of his greatest adventures.

*Shoulder articulation joint*

*Actuating coupler*

**DATA PROBE**

**UTILITY ARM**

R2-D2's computer access equipment allows him to quickly read entire networks. Known to very few, R2-D2 has been keeping internal copies of much of the data he has accessed over the decades.

### DATA FILE

> On most days, R2-D2 is kept underneath a tarp to prevent the D'Qar humidity from damaging his systems.

> R2-D2 has never had his memory wiped—a practice that dates back to Anakin Skywalker's ownership of him.

*Third tread (retracted)*

*Ankle articulation servomotor*

*Motorized all-terrain treads*

*Powerbus cables connecting power cells*

# THE SENATE

SINCE THE HISTORIC signing of the Galactic Concordance between the New Republic and the defeated Empire, the preservation of peace in the galaxy has been the dominant focus of the newly restored Galactic Senate. Convincing a war-weary galaxy that this period of renewal would be different proved challenging, as similar promises had been made during the rise of the Empire. As a bold demonstration of the government's dedication to break with historical precedent, the New Republic did not settle on Coruscant. Instead, its capital shifts across member worlds by a process of election.

Hosnian Prime serves as the current New Republic capital. Moving the Senate from Coruscant did much to convince the many disaffected systems that had tried to withdraw from the Republic prior to the Clone Wars.

Simple, modest robes of office

Signs of age respected in Tarsunt culture

Robe of assembly

Regent's turban

Surcoat of office

BRASMON KEE OF ABEDNEDO

THANLIS DEPALLO OF COMMENOR

NAHANI GILLEN OF UYTER

## CHANCELLOR VILLECHAM

A delegate from the Mid Rim Tarsunt system, Lanever Villecham is in the second year of his first term of office as Chancellor of the New Republic Senate (the word "Supreme" has been eliminated from the title). Villecham's principal concerns in office include forging more agreeable trade relations with the neutral systems of the Trans-Hydian Borderlands. He is not worried about the First Order, as long as the former Imperials are contained within their borders and are following the dictates of the Galactic Concordance.

Traditional
Ubardiani
headdress

Sash of
agreement

DATA FILE

> Despite operating with the begrudging
acknowledgment of the Senate, General Leia
Organa's Resistance movement is a wholly
independent body, whose actions are not
sanctioned by the New Republic.

> The New Republic fleet is the largest defense
force in the galaxy, but nevertheless is a
fraction of what it was during the Clone Wars.

# KORR SELLA

Leia has come to realize that her
reputation has been twisted by
corrupt politicians, and the power
of her voice has been weakened
by personal attacks and rumors
of delusion. Leia therefore relies
on Korr Sella, a young envoy,
to make her case for the
Senate to take direct
action against the
First Order.

Studied
diplomatic
demeanor

Rank of
commander

Faced with concrete evidence of the First Order's march
to war, Leia dispatches Korr Sella to the Senate, in hope
of securing military assistance from the New Republic.

Resistance
command
uniform

No-nonsense
stance exudes
authority

**GADDE
NESHURRION OF UBARDIA**

Tarisian colors
of administration

Formal
Naboo
coif

Ultraviolet
vision

Frock of the
Theed reforms

Military cut boots

**ANDRITHAL ROBB-VOTI
OF TARIS**

**THADLÉ BERENKO
OF NABOO**

**ZYGLI BRUSS
OF CANDOVANT**

# STARKILLER BASE

**HIDDEN WITHIN** the Unknown Regions that make up a vast swath of the galaxy westward of the Core is the true heart of the First Order. Concealed from the prying eyes of the New Republic and the questing probes of the Resistance, the descendants of the Galactic Empire have been amassing a power that violates the treaty restrictions of the armistice. But even their fleets of Star Destroyers and legions of stormtroopers pale in comparison to the destructive power of the First Order's newest superweapon: the sun-targeting Starkiller weapons platform.

The Starkiller is a titanic feat of engineering, and its operation requires vast amounts of personnel.

Starkiller Base is carved from the rock of an icy world, meaning that throughout the installation, mechanical surroundings give way to natural ones.

## BASE DEFENSES

Starkiller Base is the largest known deployment of First Order military forces, and yet it cannot truly be considered the headquarters of the emergent power, as Supreme Leader Snoke keeps his command center mobile. Nonetheless, legions of stormtroopers stand ready to defend the base, bolstered by TIE fighters, missile and laser batteries, and incredibly powerful planetary shields that can deflect any bombardment.

## JOINT OPERATION

The Starkiller operation is an unprecedented undertaking, requiring the efforts of every service branch of the First Order. As it has the unique characteristic of being both a planet-based and interstellar weapon, the command and operations crew draws from both Navy and Army ranks, meaning admirals and generals, commanders and majors work side by side to prime the weapon for its devastating debut.

*Coded access cylinder*

*Starkiller engineer duty uniform*

*Static-grounded boots*

**TECHNICIAN MANDETAT**

**LIEUTENANT RODINON**

*Stormtrooper executing a parade ground about-face*

*Enormous banner of the First Order*

### COLONEL DATOO

A methodical officer in charge of the primary fire control room of Starkiller Base, Colonel Datoo believes that such destructive power demands respect from all within the ranks of the First Order.

Crested command cap

### DATA FILE

> The Starkiller is the culmination of Old Empire research into dark energy translations and hyperspace tunneling.

> The First Order selected the icy world for its unique energy-transmitting crystalline deposits.

The sheer size of the Starkiller operation means that the First Order must rely on droid workers. From the polished corridors to the frozen plains, droids carry out a wide variety of essential tasks.

## STARKILLER OFFICERS

The officers of the First Order military grew up shielded on the far side of the Unknown Regions. They were the first generation to grow up after the Galactic Civil War, and with an Imperially-skewed version of galactic history. Under the guidance of Imperial veterans, they learned of a glorious past and the destiny that was stolen from them by terrorists who called themselves "rebels" and, later, the New Republic. These true believers see themselves as the only power capable of wresting the galaxy away from a path of chaos and corruption.

Commemorative band identifying Kaplan, a historic Imperial warlord

Teal army uniform

**SENTRY DROID**

Rolling casters for travel through base interior

Long-range communications antenna

**PATROL DROID**

Rey, having grown up on a desert world, is ill-prepared for the frozen planet that houses the Starkiller. With countless lives hanging in the balance, she quickly ignores any thoughts of discomfort to continue her mission.

Rey's piloting skills and mechanical instincts serve her well when she climbs behind the controls of a First Order snow speeder.

## INFILTRATION

Han Solo and Chewbacca have made a decades-long career of infiltrating seemingly impenetrable fortresses, and Starkiller Base is just the latest challenge in their path. Solo's foolhardy ingenuity lands a team of well-equipped intruders into the heart of the First Order operation, but the sheer scale of the base is unlike anything they've ever faced.

# SNOWTROOPERS

**THE IMMENSE POWER** harnessed by the Starkiller requires technology that penetrates and spans an entire planet. This means the crew and support staff of the weapon must remain mobile, zipping across and through the snow-covered globe. For security and maintenance of the Starkiller's surface facilities, the First Order equips stormtroopers with cold weather gear that is an advancement of similar equipment worn by the shock troops of the Galactic Empire. The First Order also uses such gear in the conquest of low-temperature worlds in its growing territory of space.

Polarized slit visor to minimize ice glare

Betaplast helmet with flared neck shroud

Rank pauldron

Breather tank inlets

Snowtroopers come in from the cold to examine the interior of the *Millennium Falcon* after it trespasses into First Order territory.

## GUARDING THE STARKILLER

The result of decades of searching for a world in the Unknown Regions with exacting specifications, the Starkiller planet is destined to play a crucial role in the First Order's bid for galactic dominance. As such, it is very well protected. Snowtrooper teams were the first to scout the frozen world, eliminating any native life forms that could pose a threat to the colossal excavation and construction project. Snowtroopers now guard all access points to the control headquarters, supported by patrol droids.

Utility pouch

Insulating kama

Adjustable J19 electroscope with antifogging filaments

Cooling vanes with heat shunt

Fore sight

Blaster gas valve cap

Heated filament wraps around trigger

Collapsible steadying grip

Magnatomic adhesion grip

### SONN-BLAS F-11D BLASTER RIFLE
Snowtroopers carry standard stormtrooper weaponry, with slight modifications to shunt excess heat into the more sensitive interior mechanisms.

Rugged ice boots

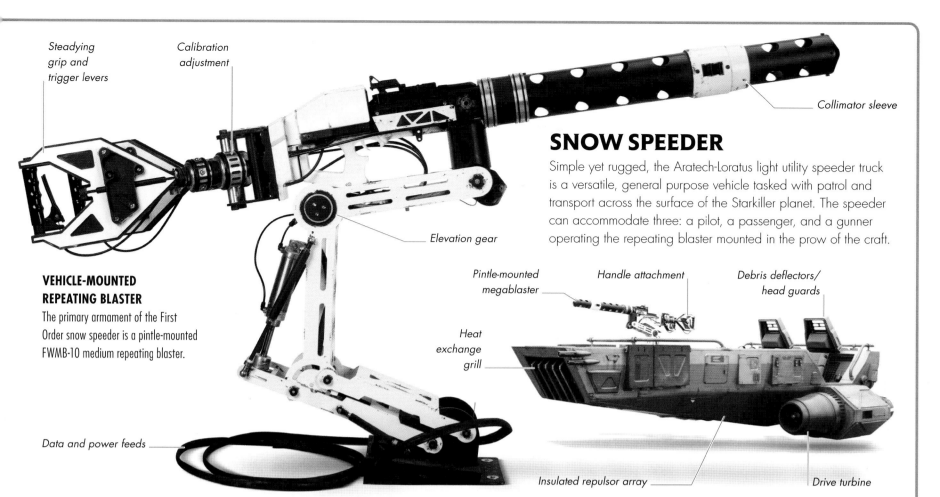

Steadying grip and trigger levers

Calibration adjustment

Collimator sleeve

## SNOW SPEEDER

Simple yet rugged, the Aratech-Loratus light utility speeder truck is a versatile, general purpose vehicle tasked with patrol and transport across the surface of the Starkiller planet. The speeder can accommodate three: a pilot, a passenger, and a gunner operating the repeating blaster mounted in the prow of the craft.

Elevation gear

### VEHICLE-MOUNTED REPEATING BLASTER

The primary armament of the First Order snow speeder is a pintle-mounted FWMB-10 medium repeating blaster.

Pintle-mounted megablaster

Handle attachment

Debris deflectors/ head guards

Heat exchange grill

Data and power feeds

Insulated repulsor array

Drive turbine

### DATA FILE

> Though the Resistance has cataloged stormtroopers equipped for cold weather, incendiary, and crowd control operations, intelligence analysts are convinced there are many more specialist units awaiting discovery.

### BODY ARMOR

The snowtrooper chest plate is made of betaplast composite, with an icephobic coating that prevents the buildup of frost, even in humid conditions.

The deep mental conditioning that First Order stormtrooper recruits undergo helps eliminate weak-willed types likely to complain about cold conditions.

## COLD WEATHER GEAR

Snowtrooper armor consists of fewer plates than the standard stormtrooper kit, to permit increased movement in difficult snow or icy terrain. However, the whole suit is sealed in an insulated "envelope," consisting of wind- and water-resistant fabric worn over a dense, heat-retaining body glove. A powerful heating and personal environment unit worn as a backpack monitors and regulates body temperature.

Braced firing stance

Unit insignia

Personal environment unit

Greave adjust straps

Suit heater controls

Insulated gloves with adjustable heating units

71

# MAZ KANATA

**DESCRIBED AS AN** acquired taste by those who know her best, the boisterous Maz Kanata has carved herself a safe haven on the fringe of the galaxy, where she holds court in an ancient castle as the preeminent font of smuggler wisdom. Kanata has goten many a young brigand started in the freebooting trade, and has a preternatural gift for sensing the shifting tides of fortune in the galaxy. She has weathered many regime changes in her long life, and has not only survived, but found ways to thrive.

*Compact weapon fits Maz's small hands*

*Power setting adjust*

**MAZ'S BLASTER**

Compelled to explore the deeper recesses of Maz's castle, Rey faces some of her deepest fears as well as an overwhelming vision brought on by the power of the Force.

*Statue of an ancient Jedi Master*

**BUST OF MASTER CHERFF MAOTA**

*Variable lens corrective goggles*

## PIRATE LEGEND

Maz's diminutive form seems at odds with her legendary exploits, though her larger-than-life personality bridges these extremes. Affable, eccentric, and wise, she has seen much in her centuries of life and can rapidly take stock of new acquaintances. In recent decades, Maz has kept secret one of her greatest strengths—an affinity for the Force. Though she has known Jedi (and has a few tall tales regarding encounters with Knights and Masters), she never walked that path herself, instead relying on her strong connection to the Force to keep her out of danger.

**FUSION CUTTER HEAD**

**DIATIUM POWER CORE**

*Bracelet of the Sutro*

*Four-thousand-year-old hyperspace sextant*

*Ancient wroshyr wood*

**MAZ'S CURIO BOX**

### MAZ'S TREASURES

In her centuries of travel, Maz has collected countless trinkets and treasures, not to sell but to protect. She has seen the tide of dark and light ebb and flow across the galaxy, and believes that a relic from the past may someday make a difference in the future.

*Socks knitted by Maz herself*

*Maz keeps the box unlocked*

*Disfigured Artiodac face*

**CHADIAN AND UBESE DRESSINGS**

*Kitchen vibro-knife*

**GORNT MEAT**

**BAKED CUSHNIPS WITH FRAL**

**MEAT TENDERIZER**

*Stained leather apron*

**FRESH FRUIT PLATTER**

### STRONO "COOKIE" TUGGS

A centuries-old fixture within the castle, Tuggs has a surly attitude that is the subject of good-natured ribbing by those who eat his cooking in the dining hall.

Thromba and Laparo are Frigosian cryptosurgeons who offer cosmetic alterations for those looking to disappear.

## MAZ'S CASTLE

Having stood at the shore of a freshwater lake for millennia, Maz's castle is a peculiar blend of ancient and current. Sensor arrays and communications gear help keep Maz connected to the wider galaxy, but a short walk from the castle plunges visitors into a primordial forest seemingly never touched by technology. Maz enjoys this contrast. To her, it is yet another manifestation of a cosmic balance.

Upon arrival at the castle, Finn, Rey, Han, and BB-8 pass by HURID-327, a jovial loadlifter droid.

### DATA FILE

> Services available at Maz's castle include appraisals, loans, medical assistance, food, room and board, games of chance, navigational updates, and basic repairs.

> Maz has only felt comfortable openly acknowledging her Force abilities since the death of the Emperor.

*Witherstring topboard*

*fingerboard and nut*

**SEVEN-STRING HALLIKSET**

*Bodhar-bone tone bars*

*Hypolliope horn cluster*

**TAYBIN RALORSA**

**INFRABLUE ZEDBEDDY COGGINS**

**UBERT "STICKS" QUARIL**

**SUDSWATER DILLIFAY GLON**

**XYLOXAN**

**KASTA DRUM**

## ENTERTAINMENT

A poet and painter, Maz delights in all forms of art as it provides a way for an old pirate to discover new wonders. She offers board to traveling musicians in exchange for their performances, and aspiring and occasionally desperate bands brave the cutthroat-filled castle. Some are thrill-seekers; others are looking to line their coffers in ventures that have little to do with music.

# MAZ'S CASTLE

**MAZ KANATA EXTENDS** a warm hospitality to those willing to abide by the unwritten rules of her castle keep. Though inevitably tempers flare and the occasional scuffle erupts from so many spacers, grifters, and pirates mingling in a small area, matters of politics and warfare must be left outside. Emissaries of galactic governments are not given any special treatment, and business trumps all matters of diplomacy and protocol. This relaxed formality has attracted a motley assortment of outlanders from all across the galaxy.

*From her vantage point on Grummgar's lap, Bazine can see all that transpires at Maz's castle tavern.*

## GRUMMGAR AND BAZINE

A big game hunter and gun-for-hire, Grummgar is obsessed with trophies, whether of the animal kind illegally poached in the wilds of distant worlds, or of the head-turning female variety attracted by his brute magnetism. Grummgar is too self-centered to consider anybody else's agenda, and does not realize that the woman he has attracted, Bazine Netal, is in fact a spy with a direct line to the First Order.

*Complex pattern is sensor-jamming baffleweave*

*Remote trigger interface*

*Sniper barrel flash suppressor*

**GRUMMGAR'S HUNTING RIFLE**

*Tough, puncture-resistant skin*

*Plastoid armor plate*

*Fierce Dowutin features include chin horns*

*Dagger coated with neurotoxic kouhun venom*

**BAZINE NETAL**

**GRUMMGAR**

*Sharp claws*

### DATA FILE

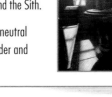

> Maz's castle is thousands of years old, and stands on land that was an ancient battleground between the Jedi and the Sith.

> As the castle is known to be neutral territory, spies from the First Order and Resistance find sanctuary there.

## WOLLIVAN

An interstellar scout and hyperspace trailblazer, the inquisitive Wollivan sells—or gambles away—valuable astrogational data and scavenged trinkets to smugglers and traders.

*Spacer's gloves*

*Blarina vac-suit*

It is hard for outsiders to tell members of the Blarina species apart. Wollivan has a large family, and when in trouble, he has more than once claimed to be the victim of mistaken identity.

*Kaleesh helmet conceals Delphidian heritage*

### CAPTAIN ITHANO

*Armorweave-lined cape*

### CAPTAIN ITHANO'S BLASTER RIFLE

*Proudly captured from a Kanjiklubber*

Desperate to find a new path in life, Finn seeks to depart Takodana with Captain Ithano and First Mate Quiggold, a pair of smugglers and pirates recommended by Maz.

*Gabdorin species*

### QUIGGOLD

*Made from hyperdrive plotter pins*

*Power plant contained in chest*

### QUIGGOLD'S PRAYER BEADS

*Hydraulic line*

### GA-97

Unassuming servant droid GA-97 is aligned with the Resistance, and plugged into their intelligence network.

*Collapsible legs for compact stowage*

*Replacement leg made from fuel funnel*

## PIRATE CREW

"Lower ye shields and come about!"—these are the terrifying orders no starship crew wants to hear over their comm. They signal the arrival of Captain Sidon Ithano, also known as the Crimson Corsair, the Blood Buccaneer, or the Red Raider. He lets his reputation, and his First Mate Quiggold, do the talking for them. They travel the starlanes in their modified freighter, the *Meson Martinet*.

# CASTLE GUESTS

## PRASTER OMMLEN

A devotee of the Sacred Ramulus, an Ithorian sect of worship, Ommlen is an Ottegan former gunrunner who has put his life of crime behind him.

*Ottegan physiology similar to Ithorian*

**WITH ITS LOCATION** in the Tashtor sector offering access to major trade routes that connect the Inner and Outer Rim, Takodana is a popular departure point for star travelers of every type. For those willing to brave the lawlessness of the sparsely settled Outer Rim or Western Reaches, Maz's castle is often the last taste of civilization. For those heading Coreward, it's a last gasp of frontier living. Fugitives desperate to avoid law enforcement have their pick of escape routes, provided they have the credits to pay for transit and the skill to negotiate proper terms.

## DIVERSE CROWD

A galaxy of different reasons brings people to Maz's castle, not all of them nefarious. Praster Ommlen, a former criminal who has now reformed, offers spiritual guidance to other criminals. Pru Sweevant robs commerce ships, while Sonsigo and Munduri are gemologists who appraise precious stones harvested on newly cataloged worlds. As different as they all may be, these beings connect, each offering something of value to another.

**PRU SWEEVANT'S BLASTER PISTOL**

*Amplified galven chamber for intense blasts*

*Blue color is camouflage in Narq's fungus forests*

### PRU SWEEVANT

A blue-faced Narquois bandit, Pru uses contacts within the Mining Guild to find out the schedules of vulnerable convoys.

Though Rey has not exactly lived a sheltered existence, Takodana holds a host of new experiences for her. Rey has never seen a world so lush, so humid, and with such a diverse population.

*Faded ascetic robes offer little comfort*

### SONSIGO AND MUNDURI

These two Bravaisian podmates are attracted to glittering gems and metals, and offer top prices.

*Goggles protect sensitive eyes*

*Measures the angle of light within gem types*

**ELECTRO REFRACTOMETER**

**PRASHEE AND CRATINUS**

Prashee and Cratinus are Ubdurian brothers who love a good game of chance, and take advantage of their identical appearance to swap identities in profitable swindles.

_Aurodium belt buckle_

_Matching Ubdurian travel smocks_

**SABACC CARDS**

_Coded value only redeemable at Maz's_

**GAMBLING CHITS**

# GAMBLING DEN

Games of chance are a popular pastime in Maz's castle as they provide a non-violent way for extremely competitive cutthroats to prove their mettle. In addition to casino classics like sabacc, pazaak, and dejarik, other popular games include Deia's Dream, a board game favored by the insectoid Dengue sisters, and droid ball fighting, wherein spheroid droids bash against each other in a square arena table, with droids of the same color being able to clump together to form more formidable fighters.

### JASHCO PHURUS
When away from Maz's castle, Jashco is a pirate who prowls the Arrowhead Region east of Coruscant.

_Field-accelerated blaster rifle_

_Tricorraan raider robes_

### HASSK TRIPLETS
Near-feral subhumanoids, these Hassk thugs are frequently itching for trouble in the main hall of Maz's castle, but other, larger beings keep the peace.

_Large eyes offer keen night vision_

_Sensitive hearing_

**CHANCE CUBES AND FIGHTING DROIDS**

_Contains valuable technology_

**PRIZE BOX**

_Flesh-tearing fangs_

## DATA FILE

> The droid ME-8D9 is rumored to be as old as Maz herself, and some believe the droid was part of the ancient castle population.

> Maz is delighted to see Han Solo again, as she has not seen the Corellian scoundrel in 25 years.

### GWELLIS BAGNORO
A mysterious Onodone who doesn't talk about his past, Gwellis is an expert forger who specializes in transit documents.

_Battered VT-33d blaster pistol_

_Izby, a pet barghest and loyal protector_

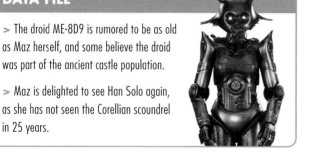

# INDEX

*Sun-shielding sedge hat*

*Scavenger's apron*

DAVAN MARAK

## A

**Admiral Ackbar** 59
**Admiral Statura** 56, 58
**Anakin Skywalker** 33, 65
**Andrithal Robb-Voti** 67
**astromech droids** 10, 11, 63, 65
**Athgar Heece** 37

## B

**Bala-Tik** 52, 53
**Battle of Endor** 8, 9, 48, 59, 60, 65
**Bazine Netal** 74
**BB-8** 10–11, 13, 22, 32, 64
*Black One* 13, 61
**blasters** 12, 15, 16, 17, 20, 23, 29, 33, 37, 39, 41, 46, 54, 55, 56, 70, 71, 72, 75, 76
**Blue Squadron** 61
**Bollie Prindell** 62

**bowcaster** 48, 49
**Brasmon Kee** 66

## C

**C-3PO** 56, 63, 64, 65
**Captain Ithano** 23, 75
**Captain Phasma** 21, 28–29
**Cherff Maota** 72
**Chewbacca** 46, 47, 48–49, 53, 69
**Chief Petty Officer Unamo** 43
**Clone Wars** 14, 16, 17, 19, 33, 40, 58, 59
**Colonel Datoo** 69
**Constable Zuvio** 36
**Core Worlds** 8, 52
**Corona Squadron** 9, 62
**Coruscant** 9, 34, 66
**Cratinus** 77
**Crokind Shand** 55
**"Crusher" Roodown** 37

## D

**dark side** 24, 26, 27
**Darth Vader** 24, 26
**Dasha Promenti** 15
**Doctor Kalonia** 48, 59
**D'Qar** 9, 56, 57, 58, 61, 62, 63, 65
**droids** 36, 43, 63, 64, 69

## E

**electrobinoculars** 62
**Ello Asty** 61
**Empire, Galactic** 8, 12, 14, 15, 16, 34, 35, 44, 52, 56, 59, 66, 70
*Eravana* 47, 50
**explosives** 23, 49

## F

*Finalizer* 24, 25, 41, 42–43
**Finn** 22–23, 32, 33, 47, 49, 50, 57, 73
**First Order** 8, 12, 13, 15, 16, 17, 20, 21, 22, 23, 25, 26, 28, 29, 32, 40, 41, 47, 49, 50, 56, 58, 60, 63, 66, 67, 69, 70, 74
    **insignia** 41
**flamethrower** 18
**flametroopers** 18–19
**FN-2187** 20–21, 23 **see also Finn**
**Force, the** 14, 15, 24, 25, 33, 47, 72

## G

**GA-97** 75
**Gadde Neshurrion** 67
**Galactic Civil War** 8, 9, 16, 34, 41, 46, 58, 60, 61, 62, 69
**Galactic Concordance** 8, 40, 41, 66
**gambling** 77
**General Hux** 28, 29, 40–41
**Goss Toowers** 62
**Grummgar** 74

**GTAW-74 "Geetaw"** 36
**Guavian Death Gang** 52–53, 54
**Gwellis Bagnoro** 77

## H

**Han Solo** 23, 33, 46–47, 48, 49, 50, 52, 53, 54, 56, 57, 69, 73, 77
**happabore** 22, 31, 36
**Hassk triplets** 77
**Hosnian Prime** 9, 66
**Hutts** 36, 54, 55

## I

**Ilco Munica** 15
*Inflictor* 35
**interrogation tools** 24

## J

**Jakku** 9, 10, 12, 14, 15, 19, 20, 21, 22, 25, 30, 31, 32, 33, 34, 35, 36, 37, 38, 59
**Jashco Phurus** 77
**Jedi** 14, 24, 26, 33, 72, 74
**Jess Pava** 61
**junkyard** 38

## K

**Kanjiklub** 54–55
**Kaydel Ko** 63
**Kelvin Ravine** 10, 14, 15
**King Prana** 50–51, 52
**Knights of Ren** 24
**Korr Sella** 67
**Kylo Ren** 12, 22, 24–27, 29, 33, 40, 42
**Kyuzo warriors** 36

## L

**Lanever Villecham, Chancellor** 66
**Leia Organa** 10, 12, 47, 56–57, 59, 63, 64, 67
**lightsaber** 26, 27, 33
**light side** 26
**Lieutenant Mitaka** 42
**Lieutenant Rodinon** 68
**Lor San Tekka** 12, 14–15
**luggabeast** 34
**Luke Skywalker** 23, 26, 33, 57, 65

DRINKS CONTAINERS FROM MAZ'S CASTLE

# INDEX

Corroded sunshield and rollbar

Steering vanes

JAKKU RAIDER SPEEDER

## M

**Major Brance** 58
**Major Ematt** 59
**Maz Kanata** 9, 33, 47, 72–73,74, 75, 77
**Maz Kanata's Castle** 73, 74–77
**medical equipment** 48, 59
*Meson Martinet* 75
*Millennium Falcon* 22, 46, 47, 48, 70
**Munduri** 76

## N

**Nahani Gillen** 66
**Nar Kanji** 54, 55
**New Republic** 8, 9, 12, 14, 16, 34, 35, 40, 41, 46, 48, 56, 57, 58, 60, 66, 67, 68, 69
**New Republic Defense Fleet** 13
**Nien Nunb** 61
**nightwatcher worm** 35
**Niima Outpost** 30, 31, 32, 34, 36–37, 38, 39
**Niima the Hutt** 36

## O

**Old Republic** 9, 16
**Outer Rim** 8, 54, 76

## P

**Palpatine, Emperor** 8, 14, 15, 28, 73
**Pamich Nerro** 63
**percussive cannon** 52
**Petty Officer Thanisson** 43
**pistols** 15, 33, 37, 46
**Poe Dameron** 10, 11, 12–13, 14, 21, 22, 23, 24, 61
**Prashee** 77
**Praster Ommlen** 76
**Pru Sweevant** 76
**PZ-4CO "Peazy"** 63

## Q

**Quadjumper** 32
**quadnoculars** 13, 16, 20
**quarterstaff** 32, 33
**Quiggold** 75

## R

**R2-D2** 64, 65
**rathtars** 50–51
*Ravager* 35, 45

**Razoo Qin-Fee** 55
**Rebel Alliance** 8, 9, 12, 13, 30, 59, 60, 62, 63
**Red Squadron** 61
**Regent Solculvis** 51
**Resistance** 8, 9, 12, 23, 32, 43, 47, 56, 57, 58, 59, 62, 65, 67, 68, 74
       command center 62–63, 64
       commanders 58–59
       ground crew 62–63
       infantry 57
       pilots 60–61
**Rey** 22, 23, 30–33, 35, 38, 39, 47, 50, 69, 72, 73, 76
**rifles** 12, 15, 37, 55, 70, 74, 75
**riot control baton** 17

## S

**salvage tools** 31, 35
**Sarco Plank** 37
**Senate, Galactic** 8, 9, 58, 66-67
**shuttle** 25
**Sith** 15, 24, 26, 74
**Snap Wexley** 60
**snowtroopers** 70–71
**Sonsigo** 76
**Special Forces** 45
**speeders** 31, 34, 63, 69
       snow speeder 69, 71
**Star Destroyer** 25, 31, 35, 39, 42, 43
**Starkiller Base** 29, 68–69
**Starkiller operation** 40, 49
**Starkiller weapon** 41, 58, 68, 70
**Starship Graveyard** 34–35
**steelpeckers** 35
**stormtroopers** 15, 16–17, 18, 19, 24, 28, 29, 40, 43, 68, 71
**Strono "Cookie" Tuggs** 73
**Super Star Destroyer** 35, 45
**Supreme Leader Snoke** 24, 25, 26, 40, 68

## T

**Takodana** 9, 23, 47, 56, 77
**Tasu Leech** 54, 55
**Technician Mandetat** 68
**Teedo** 34
**Thadlé Berenko** 67
**Thanlis Depallo** 66
**TIE fighter** 21, 32, 41, 44, 45, 68
       Special Forces 45
**TIE Pilot Corps** 44
**transports (First Order)** 17
**transports (resistance)** 57
**Tuanul Village** 15, 25

## U

**Unkar Plutt** 32, 38–39, 47
**Unknown Regions** 8, 25, 29, 34, 35, 40, 68, 69, 70

## V

**Vober Dand** 62
**Volzang Li-Thrull** 55

## W

**Western Reaches** 9, 12, 34, 76
**Wollivan** 75

## X

**X-wing** 13, 60, 61, 62

## Z

**Zygli Bruss** 67

Cybernetic arm power brace

Combat droid plate armor

ROSSER WENO

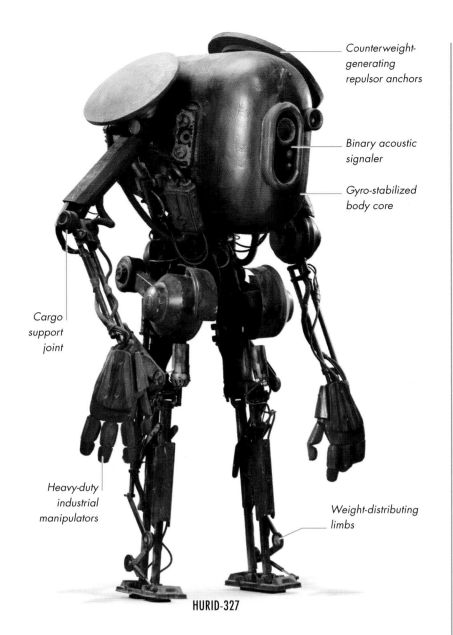

Counterweight-
generating
repulsor anchors

Binary acoustic
signaler

Gyro-stabilized
body core

Cargo
support
joint

Heavy-duty
industrial
manipulators

Weight-distributing
limbs

HURID-327

**Project Editor** David Fentiman
**Project Art Editor** Owen Bennett
**Creative Technical Support** Tom Morse
**Senior Pre-production Producer** Jennifer Murray
**Senior Producer** Alex Bell
**Managing Editor** Sadie Smith
**Managing Art Editor** Ron Stobbart
**Art Director** Lisa Lanzarini
**Publisher** Julie Ferris
**Publishing Director** Simon Beecroft

**For Lucasfilm**
**Executive Editor** Jonathan W. Rinzler
**Image Archives** Stacey Leong, Tim Mapp,
Shahana Alam, and Matthew Azeveda
**Art Director** Troy Alders
**Story Group** Leland Chee, Pablo Hidalgo, and Rayne Roberts
**Photographers** David James, Jules Heath,
John Wilson, and Shannon Kirbie

First American Edition, 2015
Published in the United States by DK Publishing
345 Hudson Street, New York, New York 10014

Page design copyright © 2015 Dorling Kindersley Limited
DK, a Division of Penguin Random House LLC
15 16 17 18 19  10 9 8 7 6 5 4 3 2 1
001—183101—December/2015

© & TM 2015 LUCASFILM LTD.

A catalog record for this book is available from the Library of Congress.

ISBN 978-1-4654-3816-4

DK books are available at special discounts when purchased in bulk for sales promotions,
premiums, fund-raising, or educational use. For details, contact: DK Publishing Special
Markets, 345 Hudson Street, New York, New York 10014
SpecialSales@dk.com

Printed and bound in the USA

A WORLD OF IDEAS:
**SEE ALL THERE IS TO KNOW**
www.dk.com
www.starwars.com

# ACKNOWLEDGMENTS

**Pablo Hidalgo:** Blazing new trails in an uncharted galaxy could be a lonely endeavor, but I've been fortunate to be surrounded by an amazing team of collaborators. To my compatriots in story development at Lucasfilm, particularly Kiri Hart, Rayne Roberts, Carrie Beck, Diana Williams, James Erskine, and Leland Chee, with whom I was witness to the genesis and evolution of *The Force Awakens*, my thanks.

I am indebted to Brian Miller, Phil Szostak, Stacey Leong, and Newell Todd for their help in navigating the flood of information that accompanies a film in production.

A trip to Pinewood Studios to witness firsthand the incredible work of the production crew—particularly the props, sets, creatures, and art department—was of immeasurable value, so my thanks to the many devoted people behind the scenes who have made the dream of a new *Star Wars* movie a reality.

This book would not be in your hands without the diligent work of J.W. Rinzler,

David Fentiman, Owen Bennett, and Sadie Smith, who not only shaped its creation but extended the invitation for me to be its author. To Jason Fry and Kemp Remillard, who are charting similar territory with their own DK *Star Wars* book, I offer my thanks.

I want to of course thank my wife, Kristen, for her support during an incredibly busy time at Lucasfilm, including now, at 4 am, when I write these acknowledgments.

I must offer my deep gratitude to JJ Abrams, Lawrence Kasdan, and Kathleen Kennedy, who not only invited me to witness the creation of this new *Star Wars* chapter, but also asked me what I thought.

And to think this is just the beginning!

**DK Publishing:** We would also like to thank Phil Szostak, Brian Miller, Natalie Kocekian, and Mike Siglain for their assistance with the creation of this book, and Joe McDonald for photographing the special fabrications.